I0540247

~~BURN~~ ~~OUT~~ TO BALANCE

5 Ways to Overcome Stress and Improve Your Well-Being at Work

JENNA HERMANS

be courageous

**Burnout to Balance: 5 Ways to Overcome Stress and
Improve Your Well-Being at Work**

Copyright © 2024 by Jenna Hermans

All rights reserved. No part of this publication may be reproduced, distributed, or transmitted in any form or by any means, including photocopying, recording, or other electronic or mechanical methods, without the prior written permission of the publisher, except in the case of brief quotations embodied in critical reviews and certain other noncommercial uses permitted by copyright law.

For permission requests, contact:
Be Courageous

jenna@bcrgs.com
www.bcrgs.com

ISBN: 9798218522148

Printed in the United States of America
First edition

To Kyle, my partner in business, love, and everywhere else.

You inspire me to be courageous every day.

Contents

My Journey in (and Out) of Burnout

I was one of those people who looked like she had her life together. For a long time, I even *felt* like I did. I had goals and achieved them. I climbed the corporate ladder, trained for triathlons, and attended grad school while working full-time. By anyone's standards, I was kicking butt. I spent time with friends and family when I wasn't working, schooling, and training, and I had energy to spare.

Until I didn't.

It seemed all of a sudden. I was hit with a tsunami-sized level of burnout, unlike anything I'd ever experienced, or even *witnessed* someone else experience. I just couldn't do it anymore.

I have a feeling you've felt this way, too. Perhaps right now, reading this introduction.

As much success and "togetherness" as I had on the surface, all I wanted to do was run far away or sleep all day. I dreamed of chucking my phone and laptop out the window, quitting my job, and starting over fresh.

I wanted to be someone with more freedom, who didn't wake up dreading the workday and counting the hours until it was time for bed. Someone with the energy to take daily walks and not snap at their loved ones and strangers on the street because they're so overwhelmed and stressed.

I made my way out of my first battle with burnout by starting over in just about every facet of my life. I quit my job, broke up with my boyfriend of three years, moved in with my mom (thanks, Mom!), and paused grad school. I took time to create a new vision for the life I wanted to live going forward and waited until I was inspired to begin again.

Thank goodness inspiration struck after a couple of months, in the form of being offered an opportunity to take over a failing preschool, where I could apply what I'd learned so far in grad school, and turn it into a thriving educational and community facility.

Shortly thereafter, I resumed grad school and met the loves of my life (my husband, Kyle, and his three children). I was fortunate to have found a partner and family with whom I could continue to build a meaningful, courageous, and fulfilling life.

As rosy as life again seemed (they never show you what happens after the "happily ever after" credits roll), I'd soon learn that burnout isn't necessarily a one-and-done. Years later I would find myself in the flames of burnout yet again.

In only 2.5 years, we moved to a new city, added a 4th child to our family, and started a new global business consultancy, Be Courageous, where Kyle would be on the road for much of the year. Becoming a birth mother, navigating parenting, and building a new community, alongside pushing forward on my career and our business goals pushed me over the edge.

As someone who identifies herself as a high-performing achiever, it was beyond frustrating that I couldn't do it all, and that made me want to not do any of it.

Of course, giving up wasn't an option. Bills had to get paid, kids had to eat. The wheels on the bus had to keep going 100 miles per hour. With my sense of self wrapped in the (false) idea that I needed to be a high-achieving professional *and* be the "best" parent ever to be valuable, I didn't see a way to cut back anywhere.

So, needing to start *somewhere* with all of my roles and responsibilities, I began with what I knew: How to manage teams and operations. I applied the skills and strategies from my Master's degree in Organizational Management, my Bachelor's degree in Psychology, and the 20 years I've worked in human resources and operations, to my home. With these methods in place, I discovered I was able to create a new sense of balance and calm amidst the chaotic nature of busy working parenthood.

Out of the ashes of this round of burnout, these strategies became the basis for my first book, *Chaos to Calm: Five Ways Busy Parents Can Break Free From Overwhelm*.

I quickly learned I wasn't the only one struggling. After *Chaos to Calm* was released, I heard from hundreds of overwhelmed parents about how my concepts helped them, and it won numerous awards in the categories of "parenting and family" and "self-help."

The concepts in the book struck a chord with nonparents as well, and professionals in various industries began asking me to speak about how to treat and prevent overwhelm in their organizations.

My mission expanded to not only support parents and caregivers but also bring these efficiencies and concepts into the workplace.

This book, *Burnout to Balance* is the sister to *Chaos to Calm*. It supports everyone in the workplace (whether in an office building, home office, or a co-working space) with the same principles of Efficiency, Habits, Communication, Community, and Self-Care.

The concepts in both books are about how to approach what brings us the most stress in our lives, differently. My approach doesn't stem from the culture we have been raised in and accustomed to—hustle, constant productivity, back-to-back, go-go-go—but instead from a sustainable, humanistic approach, providing mental models that help shift us from the way things are right now to how we prefer them to be.

Whether you're the leader of your organization, a rising leader, an entrepreneur, a solopreneur, or an entry-level employee, you'll be able to use all of the concepts in this book to help reduce your overwhelm and burnout.

And, your balance will spread beyond yourself. Your peers, employees, boss, and the leaders around you will take notice. They'll start saying, "I want what they're having!" creating more calm and balance all around you.

Transformation begins when you decide to make a change and stick to it.

For those familiar with *Chaos to Calm*, this is not just a copy with a new cover. There are some familiar concepts, but I'll show you how to apply them to your work environment. And there are new strategies as well. Achieving more calm at work, a place where you spend more than half your time will create more balance in your life.

We'll kick off with the topic of **Efficiency** talking about task, energy, and time management.

In the **Habits** chapter we'll discuss the importance of routines in your workday and how to make healthier habits and routines stick.

In **Communication**, we'll emphasize how you express yourself to others, the importance of active listening, and being proactive.

The **Community** chapter will cover the importance of connecting with your team, peers, and coworkers, as well as how to build a work community if you don't currently have one.

Lastly, you'll learn in the chapter on **Self-Care** how to take care of yourself first, so you can show up as the best version of yourself in any situation, be it a meeting with the CEO, in the boardroom, at your weekly touch-base, within a solo productive work block, or during a heated conversation about curfews with your teenager.

How calm and balance relate to each other

At first glance, one might think that calm and balance are synonymous, but with a closer look, they are two different concepts that influence each other. To be in a state of balance, you first must understand and have a relationship with your calm. If you don't have an understanding, accessibility, or self-awareness around calm, balance will not be achievable or sustained.

The relationship between calm and balance is that *calm is an internal body* state and *balance is a feeling or an outcome.*

Getting your body and mind in a state of calm creates the space for the feeling of balance. This is why the concepts of calm are intertwined throughout this book as the infrastructure for navigating through burnout.

One life

Many people think of life as either "work" or "personal," and of achieving the elusive "work-life balance." Personally, I dislike that phrase. We only have one life. It's not like you become an entirely different person when you walk through your office building's or your home's front door. You are *you,* everywhere you go. The goal is to create and sustain balance and flow across all the various parts of your life.

Everything we experience, we take with us, everywhere we go.

For example, if you had a terrible night's sleep, the ramifications aren't isolated to workplace performance. It affects your entire day, and, if you're like me, almost every interaction you have. Or, if you get in a squabble with your partner, parent, or roommate one morning, even though you may not be actively thinking about it during work, it's in the back of your mind and influential in your day.

The tools you'll learn in the pages to come will apply in both personal and professional realms.

Where to start? By learning what burnout truly is, and how it's affecting you.

All About Burnout

"Burnout is not a sign of weakness; it's a sign that you've been strong for too long."

— Anonymous

While commonalities exist in what leads a person to burnout, burnout is subjective. Everyone has different thresholds of capacity for mental and physical activities, and everyone has a different stamina. A lifestyle that works for one person may be a ticket to burnout city for another. Only you can know if you are on your way to or in burnout.

Before we continue talking about *solving* burnout, let's discuss what burnout actually *is*.

Burnout basics

Burnout is more than just feeling tired after a long day at work or having a stressful week. It's a state of chronic stress that has deep, lasting effects on your body, mind, and spirit.

Burnout = putting out fire after fire after fire, to the point of feeling scorched. You need time to recover from all the effort and energy of firefighting, but the sirens keep blaring.

Besides the fact you picked up this book, here are some clues you may be in burnout:

- *You wake up stressed, dreading your work day ahead.*
- *You feel overwhelmed by a never-ending workload.*
- *You often dream of quitting your job and running away from your responsibilities.*
- *You feel constantly drained, both emotionally and physically, no matter how much rest you get.*
- *You feel numb, disconnected, pessimistic, and even cynical about your work, or life overall.*
- *You're often irritated over minor issues.*
- *You get sick more often than you used to.*
- *You find it hard to get good sleep.*
- *You have changes (increase or decrease) in your appetite.*
- *You experience mental fog, procrastination, and reduced productivity.*
- *You avoid activities you used to love, like time with friends or going to the beach because it's just "too exhausting."*

Guess what? You're far from alone in these feelings.

- The World Health Organization (WHO) has classified "burnout" as an occupational phenomenon, and it's included in the International Classification of Diseases.[1]
- In a survey of 1,000 full-time employees, 77% reported experiencing burnout in their current jobs and 91% reported that unmanageable stress negatively impacts their work quality.[2]

Burnout happens when stress becomes so persistent that it begins to chip away at your energy, clarity, and joy. This trend of chronic stress is an epidemic and can take years off a person's life; the need for a solution to burnout is real.[3]

Without the right tools to manage stress, resolve conflicts, and set healthy boundaries, you'll find yourself spiraling into greater dysfunction, both at work and at home.

You can take comfort in knowing that how you feel now isn't permanent. Even though it may feel like there's no way out, and that burnout has caused permanent damage, there are ways to turn the burnout ship around and prevent further long-term damage. With awareness and intention, you can grab hold of the wheel of how you work and live and change direction toward a state of balance.

What happens in your body during stress and burnout

When your body experiences stress, whether for just a moment or consistently, myriad things happen in your body all at once. Your heart rate increases, breathing quickens, muscles tighten, the brain releases adrenaline and cortisol, and blood pressure rises. This is a physiological survival response to protect your body from danger, whether to prevent injury or to save your life or the life of another—resulting in a "fight-flight-or-freeze" response. This stress response has served our species well, like keeping early humans safe from hungry lions.

Fortunately, modern humans don't typically have to worry about being eaten by a predatory cat. Still, we have other stressors in our world that activate the same stress response, like car accidents, arguments with partners, getting laid off or a bad performance review, financial strain, traffic, and sick loved ones.

One of my most memorable moments of experiencing fight-flight-or-freeze (that had nothing to do with a hungry lion chasing me) was the first time I had to fire someone. It was more stressful than breaking up with a boyfriend. My blood felt like it was filled with electricity. My skin felt hot—like it was burning up from the inside. I had never let someone go before and was nervous about their reaction.

Unfortunately, I didn't prepare well beforehand, and my stressed-out state of emotions played a leading role in the termination conversation. She and I both allowed our emotions to take charge and we ended up yelling at each other. Her employment ended in a sad and disappointing way.

In the physiological state of fight-flight-or-freeze, your brain can't function properly because your body's resources are going to your essential organs, focusing on immediate survival, and not your brain for thoughtful decision-making.[4] Making thoughtful decisions in this state is extra challenging, or even impossible.

Burnout myths

Burnout is often used as a synonym for stress...but there's a difference.

Stress can be recovered from quickly, like with a cup of chamomile tea, watching a movie with your partner, taking a walk, or calling a friend to vent.

Burnout, on the other hand, lingers. It's harder to reverse burnout because it's built up over a long period.

When in a state of burnout, it can feel like there's no end in sight. It's not just a bad day at the office, or a hectic period you can "power through." It's an overwhelming sense of feeling like no matter how hard you try, you'll never catch up or find relief.

Burnout doesn't mean you're weak, lazy, incapable, or failing, but it is a signal that your energy, attention, and priorities are out of alignment. Burnout often strikes high-achievers—the ones who give everything and expect nothing less than perfection from themselves.

The opposite of burnout: Balance and flow

Balance is feeling grounded and in flow, even when life throws you challenges. It's when you're no longer living on the edge, about to fall apart. When you're grounded, it doesn't feel like a light gust of wind will blow you over. Instead, you're navigating life with more flow and ease. Stress still comes up, because, that's life, but you don't feel like you're constantly about to collapse under the pressure, and you no longer feel like throwing in the towel when a minor setback pops up.

Life's demands and your attention will never be equally spread out. **Being in balance is like yin and yang—a continuous and dynamic shifting of energy and attention where it's needed most.**

Balance is the ability to nurture the areas of your life that matter most to you on a day-by-day basis. Some days work will be more demanding and need your focus, and other days family, friends, and other commitments will require more time and attention. When in balance, you can flow between what needs your attention and energy more seamlessly without causing overwhelming stress and the feeling of running on empty. With balance, you won't be overcommitted to one aspect of your work and life at the expense of the others. It's about creating harmony among work, rest, and everything in between.

Balance is knowing how much is enough, and not expecting of yourself more than you can healthfully give.

Sounds pretty great, right!? Now that you know exactly what burnout is, let's get you to balance. At the end of the day, you deserve to feel grounded and energized—not drained and overwhelmed. Balance is the sweet spot where we all want to be.

I got myself from burnout to balance a couple of times, and I know you can, too. So, without further adieu, let's get you there.

Efficiency

Strategies and systems for streamlining performance and productivity

"We think, mistakenly, that success is the result of the amount of time we put in at work, instead of the quality of time we put in."

— *Arianna Huffington*

Efficiency and me

When I was a kid, I didn't know I had ADHD (Attention Deficit Hyperactivity Disorder). All I knew was that my mind was constantly swirling with millions of thoughts, ideas, and tasks. I had no idea where to start or how to make a decision. For example, I couldn't decide what color I wanted for my childhood bedroom, so I painted every wall a different color.

As a teen, even before a diagnosis, I developed systems of efficiency that helped me stay on track and not only complete a task but *the right task at the right time.* I took extra-long, lined Post-its and wrote down what I needed to accomplish that week: homework, projects, chores. I satisfyingly crossed off each task and item as I completed them. I added new items as the week went on. Any incomplete items at the end of the week were transferred to next week's list.

As I got older and started working, my Post-it planner moved to a Palm Pilot and continued to evolve into using the best tools and applications for organization ever since.

Throughout my 20-year professional career running Human Resources and Operations for organizations large and small, and especially in this phase of life as the COO of a global business consultancy, Be Courageous, with four kids and a traveling spouse, efficient time, task, and energy management is a necessity.

Does this sound like a typical day?

You sit down at your desk and start replying to an email, and mid-way you get a direct message from a colleague asking you to review a document due that day. So you grab your coffee cup to fill on the way to their desk. At the coffee pot (of course, it's empty, so you start another pot), you get a text from one of your kids asking if they can go to their friend's house after school. You start texting them back, just as a colleague comes up with their cup and asks the status of the project you were in the middle of emailing about before you got up. *"Ack, I never hit send,"* you think. With every step on your walk to your colleague's desk, the dread of your entire notepad of to-dos for the day makes your heart race. You haven't even had a chance to look at your list yet, filled with items like finishing this quarter's budget, onboarding a new hire, or following up on a credit card fraud alert you got when booking dinner for your anniversary. You feel your blood pressure rising and your heart starts to race, and at the same time, you're exhausted. *"Coffee, kick in please!"* you think as you greet your colleague with a labored smile.

Later, after the whirlwind of making dinner, walking the dog, and putting (and re-putting) the kids to bed, when you finally sit down, you remember the laundry has been sitting in the machine for two days, it smells like a moldy basement, and you still didn't hit *send* on that email.

The fact you're burned out is no surprise. Spending all day reacting to 1,000 urgent-feeling demands in the least efficient way possible is panic-inducing. You wish you could get ahead of your work and life, but you feel pulled along like a caboose on a runaway train.

The power of efficiency

Efficiency may not be a sexy word or concept, but it should be, because when mastered, efficiency will help give you the best life has to offer, i.e., more attention and time for the activities and people most important to you, and the space to take care of your priorities, while also improving the flow and quality of your work, keeping your deadlines, and performing at your peak. Sounds like a dream right? I promise it can be a reality; my clients and I are living proof!

Like finding the quickest route on a map instead of taking a long way around, when you create systems and build structures to streamline your time, days, weeks, etc, you'll get the most out of your time and resources. Instead of jumping from one task to another without a plan, you'll organize them in a way that gets everything done faster and with less effort.

When you're efficient, you work smarter, not harder, so you can save time, reduce stress, and have more energy both in and out of work.

In business, there are always trendy buzzwords being thrown around, like "innovation," "optimization," and "disruption." I still cringe when I hear the word "synergy" in a presentation. These words are usually used for *companies* but should be learned and adopted by individuals, as well. Companies are comprised of people, and when people have the skills and resources to optimize their workflows and have space for innovation, then so can the business.

Efficiency isn't just about how business operations, technology processes, and procedures are managed, it's about how *you* operate. How you use your time, energy, and resources best.

Being efficient and balanced at work requires streamlining at work *and* at home. We'll discuss both in this chapter. Why? Because what you do outside of work hours impacts how you show up and perform at work (anyone who has had a few too many margaritas at happy hour and showed up for work the next day can attest), and vice versa.

It's a lot easier to be fully present at work when you know your household is running smoothly and that you're not going home to a disaster. (See the Efficiency chapter in my book, "Chaos to Calm" for more on home and personal efficiency systems, tools, and techniques.)

Benefits of efficiency

While you might be able to guess what benefits you'll get by streamlining your life, here is a quick snapshot of why we're starting with this concept.

Efficiency will:

1. **Saves you time:** Efficiency is doing what you already have to do, but smarter. When tasks and time are managed efficiently, you'll save time overall, allowing you to spend more of it on what's most important to you.
2. **Lowers stress:** With a clear plan and prioritized tasks, you're less likely to feel like you're juggling too many things at once, and that "I can't do it all!" frazzled feeling.
3. **Allows your best work to shine:** When you're not rushing through tasks at the last minute, you have the capacity to do things right.
4. **Improves energy and motivation:** With clarity on what's most important to work on and when, you won't waste time and energy reacting to whatever comes your way, because

you'll know exactly what you're working on, and how and when to do it.

What to get done and when

Now that I've hopefully convinced you how optimizing your day-to-day workflow is exciting, can change your life, and reduce stress, here's how to do it.

1. Accept that not everything can be a priority at once.

As much as your boss, partner, kids, or colleagues ask from you, and as much as you want to give everyone 100%, you don't have to (and physically can't) say yes to everything. You're probably reading this book because you're stretched so thin that each person and project is only getting 1.1% of your energy and time. And that's a disservice to everyone, *especially* you.

But how do you choose what tasks to tackle and take priority over others when all of them seem so important?

2. Use your purpose to help you set your priorities.

Without a goal, intention, purpose, or mission, you'll aimlessly make decisions and waste your energy. When you know what your company's big picture mission is and what all your actions are in service of, it's a lot easier to make decisions on what to work on and when. If you're unclear about where your priorities at work should be, check in with your boss about where they want you to focus your time and energy.

Knowing your purpose removes ambivalence in decision-making. Whether it's between fixing a current product or developing a new one, you can be more proactive and productive when you know what the bigger vision is. If you're aiming to ensure your company is future-ready and not focused on products of the past, you'll prioritize energy into new product development.

My husband Kyle and I founded our business consultancy Be Courageous with one of our superpowers being helping businesses and leaders find their purpose, or, "North Star." We travel the world to help Fortune 1000 companies and startups develop clear vision, mission, and purpose statements as well as action plans to get there. *A business may have an awesome product, but what or who is it serving? What is its reason for existing? When questions come up about customers and new products, how do they know what direction to go and how to best support their customers, employees, and operations, not only for right now but for twenty years from now?* These core visionary statements help keep a company and its employees on track and streamlined toward its big goals. It's a lot easier to make business decisions both large and small when you know what your ultimate north star and goals are, and a lot easier for you, as an individual, to make decisions at work based on what that purpose is.

Does your company need to align on a purpose? *More resources here:*

Personal purpose guidance

Purpose-driven work is helpful not only on an organizational level to align teams but also on an individual level. I did purpose-work myself along with a Be Courageous coach in my early 30s and found that "to illuminate possibility" is my life purpose statement. This means that I feel my best, most empowered, and passionate when I'm in a role of supporting, guiding, and empowering others to see and activate what's possible for them. No wonder HR and coaching have been large parts of my career. If you need a guide toward your personal or professional purpose, reach out to Be Courageous at bcrgs.com.

Having a strong sense of purpose will help you make decisions about how to spend your time outside of work as well. When you live your life with your purpose and intention as your guide, you can be more efficient in your decisions in all areas of your life, from asking for a promotion or taking on new roles and responsibilities, to if you'll join the happy hour you've been invited to. *"Does this request/event/goal align with my purpose and mission?"* and *"Which of these* most *aligns with my purpose and mission?"* are questions I ask myself when I make even the simplest of decisions.

3. Use a prioritization tool (like this prioritization matrix).

When you have too many tasks on your plate, it can be difficult to know where to start. The process of filling in the matrix below helps you break down your tasks and gain focus on what's truly important. Use the matrix at the beginning of the week, whenever you feel overwhelmed by your to-do list, or when you're setting goals. The matrix is also helpful during periods of transition or change. Life transitions (such as starting a new job, moving, or other major life events) can disrupt your routine. The matrix helps you stay focused on your core values and priorities during these times to help you maintain clarity and direction.

Creating your priority matrix

With your and/or your company's purpose statement visible and in mind:

1. **Do a brain dump.** List all the tasks that are weighing on your mind. Don't judge or try to prioritize them. This space is to get everything in your mind out.

2. **Sort your tasks in the matrix below (known as the "Eisenhower matrix") based on their urgency and importance.**

Priority Matrix

	Urgent	Non-Urgent
Important		
Non-Important		

What to do with each quadrant:
Urgent + Important: DO IT.
Urgent + Not Important: DELEGATE.
Not Urgent + Important: SCHEDULE.
Not Urgent + Not Important: DELETE.

As Steve Jobs said, "Deciding what *not* to do is as important as deciding what *to* do."

3. **Create your action steps**

Based on your matrix, list the top three actions you need to focus on today or this week to align with your priorities. Use these to help you structure your weekly planner or calendar.

I created a printable priority matrix for you to download here:

Becoming a time-management ninja

We put locks on our possessions, our homes, and our cars to protect them. Why aren't we as protective about our most valuable asset, our time?

Get ready, you're about to become a ninja with time-management skills. Are you excited to see open holes in your calendar for breathing room? I'm excited to show you my #1 hack for living more efficiently.

Time blocking

Think of your calendar as a handy personal sidekick who knows all and answers all your time-related questions. Your calendar also functions as your accountability partner. It can remind you when to start your commute, when to work out, when to spend time strategizing, when to work on your board presentation, and when to pick up the cupcakes for your kid's birthday party.

If you only take one tip out of this chapter, it should be to utilize a calendar. No more double booking or not knowing when you will have time to call your doctor back, create that scope of work document, or check in with your team. You'll be able to reference your handy-dandy calendar at any moment in the palm of your hand. You will be a timekeeping superhero! *"How does she do it? She has a calendar!"*

Write everything down in an online calendar that syncs across devices. And by everything, I mean *everything*. If you don't have this mantra already, repeat after me: If it's not in the calendar, it doesn't exist. I'm serious.

Block time for:

- Checking email.
- Catching up with your boss.
- Getting the kids ready for school.

- 1x1 times with your team members.
- Creative thinking time for future projects.
- Work time (not meeting time!) to make progress on current projects.
- Time to breathe and transition in between tasks, including lunch breaks.

The beauty of buffer time

Put a cushion in between each calendar item, to plan for transition. I usually do fifteen minutes. This may sound picky and over the top, but scheduling yourself a few minutes before and after each event gives you time for the unexpected. You can use this time to think, process, and reflect on what just happened or what you need to prepare for next, not to mention a much-needed "bio break."

You can use the fifteen minutes in between tasks to think about handling a situation that's been bothering you, listen to your favorite pick-me-up song, meditate, or just close your eyes in silence. I promise it will reduce your overall stress to have cushions in your day.

When you have a solid calendar, weird things will stop popping up to hijack your day. The vast majority of those I've worked with say that having an organized and maintained calendar decreases their stress by more than half. I'll take those odds.

Anchor your day

Check your calendar at night to get mentally ready for the next day, and in the morning before starting the day to help anchor yourself. Knowing what you have going on the next day will help you prepare—like figuring out what to wear the night before (saving time in the mornings), or adjusting your alarm to accommodate whatever needs there are for the morning and day ahead.

Additionally, it's helpful to share your calendar with relevant colleagues. Everyone at Be Courageous has access to my calendar so they can see where I am and what I'm doing. They can schedule meetings without needing to ask about my availability. Having a shared or public calendar works at home as well—whether online, posted on the fridge, or both—so everyone knows what's going on and can plan accordingly.

Delegation for the win

Delegating is a time management superpower that doesn't come naturally for a lot of people, especially those who like to control every part of the process. I understand the desire for this, but to reduce burnout and achieve balance, figuring out who besides you can take on certain tasks and responsibilities is key.

We already talked about how to prioritize tasks. You have priorities that are most important to you—maybe your family, career, physical and emotional health, financial stability, independence, fun and recreation, friendship, personal growth and development, sustainability, community, social action, and/or hobbies. For items and tasks that aren't as important (on the Urgent + Not Important and/or Not Urgent + Not Important quadrants of the priority matrix), outsource them.

If a task conflicts with your purpose, delegate it, outsource it, or erase it from your list. Maybe a colleague asks if you can support them on a project they're doing, and you get asked to drive your son's best friend to soccer practice twice a week. The added work would mean you'd have to work longer, and the carpool travel would mean you'd have to leave work early a couple of times a week.

Initially, you want to say yes to both (both seem important!) but look at the priorities that match your purpose. Does doing either or both of these line up with your core priorities, or do they conflict?

One of your priorities could be building rapport and team building at your work. Knowing this makes it easier to say 'yes' to the colleague and 'no' to the driving request. You can kindly say, *"I really wish I could, but I don't have the bandwidth right now. You could ask Stacy. I heard she's looking for soccer carpool partners."*

Or, perhaps your bigger priority is to build and nurture community in your personal life (community is a huge part of balance as you'll see in the upcoming chapter, "Community"). If your personal community is the bigger priority (like it was for me when I moved to a new town), it helps you say to the colleague, *"Now isn't a great time to take on the extra work, but I'll have more space in a few weeks (after soccer season!)."*

Creating a productive work environment

Some people love a fully expressed desk, filled with as much sentimental decor as possible, and others work best in a minimalist space. Your desk space, whether you have a little or a lot, needs to be organized and intentional to streamline your work.

Here's how to create a workspace that enhances focus and minimizes interruptions.

Unnecessary time spent finding a stapler or stack of Post-its could be spent on a quick brain break or other tasks. Every item on your desk and in your workspace should have a home, and it should always return to its home after use.

Is your workspace conducive to the type of work you need to perform? Your area should be organized to support your daily tasks. Keep frequently used items within arm's reach while storing less-used items out of sight to reduce visual clutter.

- **Minimize visual distractions**

Visual clutter can be one of the biggest culprits in derailing your focus. Limit the number of items on your desk to only what is essential.

Your physical space influences and represents your mental space. When your physical space is tidy and streamlined, the mind can more easily follow suit. When your physical space is cluttered, the mind is often as well.

Physical clutter not only takes up physical space, it takes up mental space. Have you ever experienced the satisfaction and sense of accomplishment after decluttering, purging, organizing, or cleaning? It could be as small as clearing out a single drawer or individual shelf, or as large as a whole room or car deep clean.

Few actions give me the same sense of satisfaction and joy as tidying a disorganized area. There is a natural ease that happens when spaces are tidy. Like walking into a fresh hotel room before you've unpacked—it has just the basics and is clean and neat. Or a home that's been staged for selling.

Creativity more easily flows (for most people, not all) when there's openness and spaciousness.[5] There is literal and metaphysical space for potential and creativity when there is *space.*

- **Control noise levels**

Noise is another common distraction at work. If you work in a shared or open-plan office, noise-canceling headphones can be a game changer. Alternatively, create a playlist of instrumental music or ambient sounds that help you focus. You could also listen to binaural beats, which have been shown in studies to reduce anxiety by 26%.[6] Or you can wear noise-canceling headphones or good old-fashioned earplugs for some basic and simple silence. That's my go-to, especially while writing.

For those working from home, establishing boundaries with family members or roommates about noise levels during work hours can help maintain a quiet environment conducive to concentration.

- **Manage digital distractions**

In addition to visual distractions, we have even more competition for digital attention. It's easy to have your flow disrupted and be pulled away from a productive work block with incessant notifications, emails, and social media.

Design your digital workspace to reduce these distractions. This includes turning off non-essential notifications, using apps that block distracting websites during work hours, setting specific times to check email or pausing your inbox (there are myriad installable plug-ins), and utilizing the "do not disturb" function on your devices. By controlling the flow of incoming digital information and notifications, you can create a more focused work environment.

There's a statement in my email signature saying that I work in time blocks and check email infrequently so I can be most productive throughout the day. It says:

> "A note on email responses: I work in blocks of time to be more productive, so I only check email twice daily on weekdays (once in the morning, and once in the afternoon), but I will get back to you as soon as I can. This makes more time for creating meaningful content and serving awesome people like you! I answer ALL my email inquiries, so sit tight, I'll be back soon!

Distractions create the same inefficiency effect as multitasking (mentioned later in this chapter).

Every time we get distracted from a task there's "mental lag time" which describes the amount of time it takes to resume a task and the cognitive cost associated with interruptions on work and productivity. As found in a study titled "*The Cost of Interrupted Work: More Speed and Stress*[7]," there's a resumption lag averaging 23 minutes and 15 seconds before returning to the original task. This time includes dealing with the interruption and any follow-up tasks that arise from it.

Additionally, the study found an increase in error rates when interrupted and then resumed, increased stress, and a higher perceived workload when interrupted.

In a nutshell, interruptions = lost time and increased stress.

- **Get comfy**

Did you know that your physical comfort is directly linked to your ability to focus?[8] Invest in ergonomic furniture that supports your body. When you're comfortable, you won't need as many breaks to relieve yourself and will be better able to maintain focus and sustain higher productivity levels throughout the day.

This can include a chair that provides proper lumbar support, and/or alternating with a ball chair or standing desk if space and budget permit. A desk at the correct height for your arms and elbows, and a monitor positioned at eye level to reduce strain, all contribute to physical comfort and increased focus.

- **Light it up**

Proper lighting reduces eye strain and maintains focus. Natural light is ideal, so position your workspace near a window if possible. If natural light isn't available, use a desk lamp with adjustable brightness. When I used to work in an office building without access to natural light, I loved changing my lamp settings throughout the day to match the natural cadence of the day's sunlight. And, when possible, avoid harsh overhead lighting, which can cause headaches and fatigue.

- **Bring the outside in**

Bringing elements of nature into your workspace can have a calming effect and improve concentration. This can be as simple as adding a plant to your desk or placing a small water feature nearby. Studies have shown that incorporating natural elements into your workspace can reduce stress and enhance focus, helping you feel more peaceful and calm throughout the day.[9]

Think about when you go for a hike or to the beach, visiting mountains, lakes, and forests, and how grounded and less stressed you feel. There's a reason you're drawn to nature—you need it! Humans are part of the natural world, and our current environment is an evolutionary mismatch.[10]

If you have a green thumb, get plants you can tend to. When I get stressed, one of my favorite things is to prune and water my plants. It gives me something to focus on that is in my realm of control, I feel productive, and connected with nature, and I see that my efforts and nurturing are appreciated as I witness the plants' growth.

Fake greenery will do the job, but real is better if possible. Another study showed that in the hospital, patients recover more quickly when they have a view of nature.[11] Exposure to nature is that powerful!

- **Personalize, thoughtfully**

While it's important to minimize clutter (as we established in minimizing visual distractions), **it's equally important to personalize your workspace in a way that inspires you.** This might include a vision board, motivational quotes, or objects that remind you of your goals. We've all seen it in a TV show or movie, a person working tirelessly at their desk looks over at a picture of their family or a meaningful message, and they return to work with a renewed sense of purpose and determination.

These personal touches can serve as gentle reminders of why you do what you do, providing motivation and focus when you need it most. Include a natural, calming, and joyful item or items in your space. A reminder of a trip you loved, a picture of a loved one, artwork made by one of your kids, or an image of a goal you're trying to achieve.

Energy efficiency

Efficiency in the workplace is directly linked to how well you manage your energy. When you're low on energy, slumped in your chair like a sloth, it's a lot harder to be efficient with your time and tasks. When your energy is up, you're able to knock down tasks like bowling ball pins.

Most people *think* they understand the concept of energy and how to navigate their energy cycles. *"I'm feeling low energy right now, so I'll drink some coffee and eat a granola bar to get back into the groove."*

That's all well and good, but there's a lot more to harnessing and navigating your energy to enhance your effectiveness and performance than that. When it comes to energy, as with most concepts, knowledge is power.

The best first step is to gain an understanding of your natural energy flows and what gives and takes your energy.

Recognizing the ebb and flow of your energy throughout the day enables you to structure your work accordingly. For example, scheduling high-focus, heavy-thinking work during your peak energy hours and reserving less demanding tasks for when your energy dips can help you maintain a steady level of productivity without overexerting yourself.

Elements of energy

Energy isn't just physical; it encompasses mental, emotional, and even spiritual aspects. *Mental energy* relates to your ability to focus and think clearly, while *emotional energy* is tied to your mood and resilience. Energy can be gained and expelled in these ways as well. They're interconnected. If you support one, it directly affects another. When understood as separate elements, you'll be better equipped to notice where you get drained and what fills it up.

Emotional energy

As you know, your emotional state can make or break your day. Negative emotions, such as stress, anxiety, and frustration, can drain your energy quickly. On the other hand, positive emotions, such as enthusiasm and gratitude, can boost your energy and resilience.

- **Mindfulness and relaxation techniques:** Practices such as meditation, deep breathing, and mindfulness can help manage stress and replenish mental energy, helping you maintain focus and calm throughout the day.
- **Set boundaries:** Protect your emotional energy by setting clear boundaries around your time and workload. You can do this by saying no to unnecessary commitments and delegating tasks to prevent unnecessary energy depletion.

Spiritual energy

Spiritual energy comes from doing work that aligns with your values and sense of purpose. When your work feels meaningful, it naturally generates energy and motivation, making it easier to stay engaged. Reflecting on the "why" behind your tasks (which we talked about above with priorities) can ignite your passion and provide the energy needed to sustain long-term productivity.

Physical energy

Prioritizing night-time sleep

You've heard it before, but I'll say it again because the cliche is true. **Quality sleep is one of the most critical factors in maintaining and sustaining energy.** Lack of sleep not only reduces physical energy but makes it harder to focus and perform effectively.

As you know, when you don't get enough sleep, or your sleep is interrupted (parents know all about this!), you aren't able to show up as your most creative, supportive, patient self. Even easy tasks seem difficult, and you certainly can't maximize efficiency in a sleep-deprived stupor.

There are major bodily activities and repairs that happen during sleep, such as the repair of vital organs and detoxification, among many other important functions that affect your energy.[12]

In addition to just being straight-up cranky, not enough sleep affects your mental health. Lack of sleep can increase anxiety and depression.[13] Both of those are obvious burnout promoters.

Prioritizing sleep helps you be more efficient because when you're sufficiently rested, it takes you less time to do hard tasks, and it makes hard tasks easier and less stressful.

Fueling your body

You probably already know this, but just in case you don't realize the significance: **A balanced diet that includes a mix of complex carbohydrates, protein, and healthy fats can provide sustained energy throughout the day.** I love eating a sweet treat in the afternoons, but I'm discerning of what I eat and when, because high-sugar snacks can lead to energy crashes and decreased efficiency. Most people know what food alterations they need to make to feel better and more energetic, but it can sometimes feel too hard to change a habit (see chapter on Habits for help on this.)

When you have a stacked day and need all the energy you can get, it's best to stay away from pastries for breakfast and candy bars for afternoon snacks. I'm not saying to never eat sweets, but rather to be choosy and thoughtful about when and the amounts, based on what you have going on for the day. The practice I live by is "everything in moderation." You'll often find me treating myself on Friday afternoons since I already have a natural energy dip at the end of the week—I figure, it's Friday, so why not celebrate all the hard work I did and indulge a bit? One of my clients saves her weekly fancy-and-loaded-with-sugar latte for Fridays, and you should see her face when she sips it. She looks like the famous scene of Meg Ryan in the movie *When Harry Met Sally*. She's in heaven! Which wouldn't be the same if she indulged every day.

It's easier to feed yourself well when you're proactive than reactive. Prepare for what you'll eat versus making decisions in real time. When hungry (or hangry!), you'll tend to reach for whatever's closest. But when you've proactively prepared food for yourself the night before or the morning of, you're less likely to go for the instant gratification of brownies in the breakroom, fast food around the corner, or ordering take-out with a colleague. You'll eat what you've prepared, saving you time (and money).

Being proactive with your meals also makes it easier for your future self. If you made a grab-and-go lunch, you won't have to think about what you're going to eat at lunchtime, saving your decision-making energy for work tasks, not lunch—a welcomed deposit into your time bank account.

Exercise

Regular exercise boosts energy levels.[14] Even short bursts of physical activity during the day can increase blood flow and oxygen to the brain, enhancing focus and mental clarity. This is one of the reasons why smartwatches alert you when you've been sitting for too long.

Even when you feel sluggish and don't want to exercise, moving your body even just a little bit will increase your energy. It seems counterintuitive because obviously, a good workout makes you feel "tired," but research and personal experience prove that exercising pays off with increased energy for the rest of the day and in the long run with regular practice.[15]

Exercise is incredibly efficient; it's a one-stop shop that improves so many facets of the body, mind, and spirit. Moving your body increases endorphin levels and stimulates the release of other feel-good chemicals in the brain.[14] It also boosts heart health, improves sleep, sharpens the mind, and promotes mental focus. If just thirty minutes of sweating a day can do all that; that's insurance I'm willing to pay for!

How hormones affect energy

Get your big-kid pants on now, we're going to kick off our discussion on the elements of energy by going over a topic that makes some people squirm (even though it should be totally normalized, it's just biology). Hormones play a significant role in regulating energy levels, mood, and overall well-being, influencing how you perform at work and manage stress. Understanding how your hormone cycle affects you can provide insights into optimizing your energy.

Understanding hormonal cycles in women

If you didn't cover it in biology or sex ed, women experience cyclical hormonal changes throughout their menstrual cycle, which typically lasts around 28 days but can vary widely.

- During the **follicular phase (Days 1-14)** a woman's body is gearing up to ovulate. Estrogen levels rise which can give women more energy and better moods, making motivation and focus easier to come by.

  This is a great time for working on complex tasks, creative projects, and high-energy activities (schedule the pickleball tournament you want to play during this time!) I feel like a superhero during the follicular phase—throw anything my way and I'll knock it out of the park!

- After ovulation (a quick 24-48 hour event occurring on day 14), the **luteal phase (days 15-28)**, brings inconsistent energy levels. The body is preparing for a possible pregnancy and goes into energy preservation mode. Some women experience varying degrees of physical discomfort (cramping, digestive issues) and symptoms like fatigue, irritability, and difficulty concentrating.

  This phase is better suited for tasks that require less intense focus and are more flexible. If you control your workflow at your job or run your own business, try not to schedule your most challenging work during this time.

Men have hormone cycles, too

Yes, guys, you have hormone cycles, too! They are less pronounced but still impactful. The most significant cycle is the daily fluctuation of testosterone[16]:

- **Morning peak:** Testosterone levels are highest in the morning, meaning peak energy and focus. Men typically feel their mightiest in the mornings, and are the most productive and motivated during the early hours, making this the best time for presentations, team brainstorming, high-priority tasks, decision-making, and digging into the problems you may have been putting off.
- **Afternoon decline:** As the day progresses, testosterone gradually decreases, leading to lower energy. Afternoons are best for routine tasks or administrative work.

Efficiency obstacles

Efficiency obstacle #1: Multitasking

Multitasking is a skill that many think they should be better at. Leaders and high-performers know how to "do it all," probably *too* well. We're great at it . . . until our minds explode. At work, we often multitask in situations we shouldn't, and it greatly affects our ability to be efficient.

Most of the time multitasking is an efficiency killer because the mind can't focus on two thought processes at once, at least not well. Bouncing between two ideas that require significant thought takes longer than if each one was done individually. Research has found that shifting between tasks can cause a delay as the mind takes time to "shift gears" and also results in errors because of a reduction in accuracy, which ultimately makes the process less efficient than working on one task at a time.[17]

The way to know when it's appropriate to multitask is to think about the brain power needed for each task or idea. Never multitask while needing to be attentive and thoughtful.

For example, suppose you try to compose a work presentation while helping with your daughter's homework. What could have taken you one hour will now most likely take multiple, and will include the frustration of constant interruptions to your flow, plus the potential breakdown of rapport with your daughter when she asks for your attention on a question and you keep saying, "Just a moment, I need to finish this slide." *cringe*. Those are competing tasks that both require your full attention.

Multitasking your self-care can be a big win, though. If your commute is biking distance, ride to work or to your kids' school at pickup to get your workout in. I rode my bike to work while training for my first triathlon and never had to train on the bike outside of that. On Sundays, I love wearing a face mask while folding laundry and listening to an audiobook - it's a multitasking trifecta!

Multitask when the stakes are low and the brain power needed is even lower. Listening to a true crime podcast while chopping up veggies: Yes! Compiling work emails while on the phone with your mom during your weekly catch-up: No!

Efficiency obstacle #2: Procrastination

My Grandpa Saul, an efficiency wizard, and the most responsible and generous human I've ever known, always used to say, *"Don't push to tomorrow what you can do today."*

Think about how you spend your time as if minutes and hours were deposits and debits into an interest-bearing "future-self bank account." What you efficiently accomplish now is like a deposit, granting you more time later. When inefficiently multi-tasking, you are wasting precious time, and taking debits out of the account. Efficiency, when practiced consistently, has compounded interest.

For example, if you get home from a work trip at a decent hour on a Sunday, unpack, run the laundry, and fold while watching a movie or your favorite guilty pleasure show. This way you reap the benefits of a full wardrobe for the week ahead, as well as lightening your mental load of knowing you need to do extra laundry during your already very busy and full work week.

For tasks that must get done even when you're exhausted, try to get them over with as soon as possible. Certain (more mindless) tasks are best to do as soon as possible to wipe them from your mental load, like responding quickly to a colleague if you can attend the next team offsite. It takes little mental power to look at your calendar to see your availability. Your future self will thank you!

Efficiency obstacle #3: Decision-making fatigue

Decision-making fatigue occurs when the mental energy required to make choices becomes depleted after a series of decisions, leading to poorer quality decisions as the day progresses. This mental exhaustion is closely linked to burnout, as the constant demand for cognitive resources can lead to chronic stress and emotional drain.

Prolific investor Warren Buffet has said that his job is to *"sit in a room and think,"* and that he makes *"maybe three or four really good decisions a year."* Jeff Bezos also famously said, *"If I make, like, three good decisions a day, that's enough."* Supported by psychologist Roy F. Baumeister, decision-making is mentally exhausting and our ability to make good choices diminishes as we make more decisions, especially later in the day.[18]

This is your permission to be selective with the number of decisions you need to make in a day – quality over quantity is the key to avoiding decision-making fatigue.

Strategies to combat decision-making fatigue:

- **Prioritize:** Focus on the most important decisions and delegate or automate the rest. Make your most meaningful and important decisions earlier in the day. For example, don't use important work-related thinking time in the late morning to decide on what takeout to order for dinner that night. Revisit the above section on priorities for more detail.
- **Simplify:** Reduce choices by creating routines and establishing boundaries. For example, perhaps a sales manager simplifies the decision-making process by establishing a routine for lead follow-up, deciding that all high-priority leads will be contacted within 24 hours, medium-priority leads within 48 hours, and low-priority leads at the end of the week. This routine eliminates the need to constantly reassess which leads to contact next, freeing up brain power for more important decisions, like negotiating deals.
- **Take breaks:** Regular breaks, even small ones, help reset your mind, allowing you to return to decision-making tasks with greater clarity.
- **Batch decisions:** Group similar decisions together to minimize mental switching and reduce cognitive load. For example, an HR manager could batch similar tasks like reviewing job applications and scheduling interviews. By dedicating specific blocks of time to these tasks, they avoid the mental strain of switching between different types of work, making the process more efficient and less exhausting.

- **Delegate:** And again, when appropriate, delegate. A CEO might delegate the decision of which software to implement to the IT team, trusting their expertise. By doing so, the CEO conserves mental energy for strategic decisions like mergers or market expansion.
- **Write it down:** Instead of holding all of the thoughts, tasks, and ideas in your brain, write them down when they come to mind. This way their importance is captured, and your mental load is lightened.
- **Schedule it:** Put time on the calendar to think about or make decisions about the various items in your mental load, even if it's ten minutes from now. A project manager might block out time each morning to review and prioritize tasks for the day. By scheduling this decision-making time, they avoid making hasty decisions under pressure and ensure each task is thoughtfully considered.

Efficiency obstacle #4: Martyr Syndrome

Martyr Syndrome occurs when you take on excessive workloads, refuse to delegate, and sacrifice personal well-being, so you can be seen as indispensable. While this behavior may seem admirable and come from a place of positive intent, it often leads to unnecessary chronic stress and emotional exhaustion.

At the expense of our health and desires, high-performers will do things like stay up late because we volunteered for an extra project believing perhaps that we are the only ones who can get things done correctly. This doesn't work for the long-term as taking on extra projects, working late into the night, and rarely taking time off leads to exhaustion, resentfulness, overwhelm, and dips in productivity despite working harder. All of this leads to, you guessed it, burnout.

Here's how to avoid Martyr Syndrome:

- **Set boundaries:** Establish limits between professional and personal life. i.e., don't check your work email when you wake up in the middle of the night to pee, and instead cuddle with your dog or partner after your bathroom interlude.
- **Delegate tasks:** Trust others to handle responsibilities. You probably work with or have hired capable, smart people. Let them pitch in.
- **Shift your mindset:** Understand that taking care of yourself by not burning the candle at both ends enhances productivity. Give yourself a pep talk to remind you of the big picture and that martyring yourself doesn't actually benefit anyone.

Efficiency Obstacle #5: Lack of self-care

Self-care is so important that there's a whole portion of this book dedicated to this topic. But here's how it relates to efficiency: By not taking care of your basic physical, mental, and spiritual needs you are susceptible to your energy being hijacked and not being able to be efficient with your time and energy.

Life and all its components, whether at work or home, are harder to handle with little, or inconsistent self-care. When you're caring for your body, mind, and spirit, challenges are surmountable, and patience and focus are higher. More on this soon.

Sustainable energy practices

Take regular breaks

Short (as little as 5 minutes) regular breaks throughout the day can help replenish your mental and physical energy. These breaks prevent the mental fatigue that can build up when you try to push through long periods of work without rest.

We all like to think we're invincible at work—cranking out emails, solving problems, and tackling to-do lists like a superhero swooping in to save the day. Taking regular breaks isn't just a luxury—it's a necessity. Even superheroes need a break. Imagine Batman trying to fight crime after skipping his mid-day snack break; he'd probably end up napping in the Batmobile or hangrily snapping at the victim he's saving. Just like caped crusaders, we mere mortals too need to recharge our batteries to keep performing at our best.

Research shows that short, regular breaks increase productivity, boost creativity, and help maintain focus.[19] Sometimes, the best ideas come when you're not actively thinking about the problem at hand. Sherlock Holmes might have solved his toughest cases after a leisurely stroll through the park or a cup of tea by the fireplace. When you give your brain a break, it has time to process information in the background. This is when those "Eureka!" moments happen—like realizing the solution to that complex report might just be hiding in plain sight. This is why so many great ideas come to us while we're in the shower.

So, next time you're tempted to push through lunch, remember that even Wonder Woman needs to recharge her lasso.

The Pomodoro Technique: Because tomatoes aren't just for salads

Ever heard of the Pomodoro Technique? It's a time management method that involves working in 25-minute bursts followed by a 5-minute break. The name comes from those tomato-shaped kitchen timers—because, apparently, someone decided that tomatoes are the ultimate symbol of productivity. But, hey, it works! After four "Pomodoros," take a longer break (15-30 minutes). To best use this method, choose the task(s) you are going to focus on, then set your timer, and go!

Napping: It's not just for cats

Let's talk about the afternoon crash; the time of day your energy dips and you start fantasizing about taking a nap under your desk like a snoozing cat. A quick power nap or a relaxing break can help reboot your energy levels. Studies suggest that even a 10-20-minute nap can improve alertness and performance.[20] So, if you can sneak in a siesta, go for it—just set an alarm so you don't sleep through your next meeting.

Comedy as a remedy

Breaks don't have to be just about resting; they can also be about having a little fun. Take a few minutes to watch a funny video, share a joke with a colleague, or read something that makes you smile. Laughter is a great stress reliever and can give you the boost you need to tackle the rest of your day.

More energy tips

Anchor your energy before and after energy-sucking tasks

If you know the company all-hands meeting is the most soul-sucking 90 minutes of your month, get prepared by doing something that fills your cup directly before and/or after the meeting. That way, you will be filled with good feelings going into the energy-depleting experience and/or anticipate something joyous to look forward to afterward.

Self-awareness of your energy

If you haven't noticed what your energy givers or takers are, start paying attention. *Do you get energy from a big meeting with lots of participation or sitting in a quiet corner researching? At what times?* Learn how to read your body and mind's energy clues by paying attention to the natural rises and falls, and then play with what works and doesn't during those moments, which will help you make the most efficient use of your time.

Capitalize on your natural energy moments

Schedule tasks that require the most brain or physical power on days and times you feel most focused and energetic (see the above section on hormones for a start). Don't schedule energy-draining tasks during times you know you'll be depleted.

What if you feel like you don't have *any* energy *anytime?* Oh yes, I hear you. I have four kids and a partner who travels out of the country regularly. But in your no-energy life, you probably still have times when you have a little more energy than not. Take note of those times.

Look at the small, tiny things you can do. And respect your right to say, "I'm a no for this time, thanks though," when optional requests that could overwhelm you come in. You own the calendar. Build it in. You can create an environment that allows you to have downtime.

Pro tip: Creating an energy-friendly workplace culture

It may sound unconventional and bold and takes thoughtful coordination, but workplace policies and culture can be adapted to accommodate employees' energy cycles. You can start this movement by leading by example, planning your work according to your own energy cycles, and encouraging open dialogue. Create a culture where you and your team feel comfortable discussing energy levels and the potential need for flexibility. I'm not saying everyone should share their menstrual cycle calendars with their colleagues, but trusting a colleague or employee's positive intent in managing their schedule to coincide with their energy goes a long way.

Efficiency wrap-up

Efficient practices and attention to energy will help you get more done quickly *and* create more space and energy to spend on the things you *want* to do, and not just things you *have to* do, which all contribute to your goal of feeling balanced and reducing burnout.

√ **Monitor your energy.** Everything you do gives and takes energy. Maximize complex tasks and thinking activities when energy is high, reserving more automated tasks for when energy is low.

√ **Physical energy.** Be aware of the physical elements that take or give you energy. They are sleep, food, exercise, and hormonal cycles.

√ **Use your calendar.** Put everything (everything!) into your calendar, including time cushions.

√ **Delegate.** Outsource tasks that aren't necessary for you to do, especially when someone else can do them better and faster (and may care more!).

√ **Do one thing at a time.** Don't try to multitask when one or more items need thoughtful attention.

You now have all the tools needed to increase your efficiency by prioritizing and streamlining your to-dos and tasks as smoothly, quickly, and time-effectively as possible to enhance your balance. With all of the time and energy you'll save, how about focusing on some healthy habits? That chapter is next.

Habits

Small and simple routines that have lasting effects

"We are what we repeatedly do. Excellence, then, is not an act, but a habit."

— Aristotle

The lowdown on habits

Some days you feel like you're on fire. Unstoppable. Ideas are flowing. You're taking the world by storm. On other days, the morning alarm goes off and you moan, "Noooo." Sluggish, in a daze, and slumped in your chair, you get the bare minimum done, counting the minutes until you can put on your jammies and get back into bed.

Motivation and inspiration are powerful for stimulating action, but they can wax and wane. There are days when energy and willpower are high and other days when they are nowhere to be found.

We've all been there. We make a sweeping proclamation, like, *"I'm going to read one business book every month," "I'm only going to drink alcohol on the weekends," "I'll do more networking on LinkedIn,"* or, *"I'm going to take a walk every day."*

These are all great goals, but most of the time, just like with New Year's resolutions, as soon as the novelty wears off, so does the consistency, and you're right back where you started. So, how do you keep your commitment to yourself and reach your goals when your motivation has vanished?

This is where the power of habits comes into play. With a solid habit, tasks become as instinctual and nonnegotiable as brushing your teeth or turning off the lights when you exit a room. You don't need willpower or inspiration to grab your keys before you leave home; you just do it.

Being intentional about building habits that streamline your tasks and responsibilities can make your day run more smoothly and with less stress. For example, I developed the habit of organizing my workspace at the end of each day, so that when I start the next day, I can dive straight into work without wasting time getting situated or searching for what I need.

It may seem small, but as you'll learn later in this chapter, micro-habits add up to big gains over time. As you read on, I'll guide you on how to build the infrastructure you'll need to establish and maintain healthy habits that support your overall balance and well-being.

Want to know the best part? **Unlike your past New Year's resolutions, your new habits will stick because you won't be overcommitting, setting unrealistic goals, or setting yourself up for failure.** In times of low energy or stress, even if you think "I don't want to do it." you'll simply will because:

1. You know it'll feel good to have done it, and
2. It will be as ingrained as checking your email in the morning or locking your door when you leave the house.

You might be wondering, *"Where do I begin?"* Good news! You already have. You're working your way through this book, and you're already on the right path by reflecting on your current habits and seeking to improve them for a more balanced life.

What's a habit?

Understanding how and why habits are formed will make building and sustaining them more effective and successful.

Habits are behaviors, thoughts, and actions you do instinctually, without conscious thought.

Some examples of habits:

- Logging into your computer as soon as you sit at your desk.
- Locking your car or front door.
- Checking your phone while standing in line.
- Taking your shoes off before walking inside.
- Assuming someone is mad or upset when their messages to you are short.
- Awkwardly saying, "You too!" when a cashier says, "Enjoy your movie" (and then thinking, *"They're not going to the movie, why did I say that?"*)

Because habits are automatic behaviors that have become a natural part of your routine and are practiced regularly, they become difficult to give up, and you feel strange if you don't do them. If you always get a coffee before sitting at your desk, and one morning you rush to your desk for a video call without your coffee, it'll likely feel like something is out of place or not quite right. Or if you are used to going to the gym on your way home, and one day you have to go straight to an event instead, it'll probably feel weird not having your gym bag with you and commuting there after work.

Habits can make or break balance

Habits are the foundation of routines that can give or take energy throughout the day. Without having a solid habits foundation to rely on, we're prisoners to what happens to us, forced to react to everything that comes our way.

I believe that life (and success) is the result of our habits. Jack Canfield, author of over 150 books, motivational speaker, and corporate trainer said, *"Your habits will determine your future."* He couldn't be more correct. Brian Tracy (motivational speaker, author of over 70 books, and researcher), also said *"Successful people are simply those with successful habits."*

The bottom line is that what we do regularly influences who we are now and in the future. This is why learning how to build good habits (and break bad ones) is an essential life skill with widespread benefits, including less stress and more resilience.

Creating healthy habits and trashing the crappy ones

When we consider starting a new habit, it often begins with a big, ambitious, and often vague goal. "I'm going to lose 50 pounds," "I'm going to read a ton of books this year," "I'm going to double our sales this quarter," or, "I'm going to stop wasting so much time scrolling on social media."

These are fantastic proclamations, but typically, most people set them with little or no upfront planning. Without working through the details and creating habits to support your goal, it's doomed to fail.

If you want your goal of balance to stick, you'll need to address common obstacles, such as:

- Setting goals that are too broad and too big in scope.
- Lacking a plan with detailed and specific strategies and tactics.
- Missing essential resources necessary for the goal's success.
- Failing to establish accountability.

I share how to mitigate these challenges and more throughout the remainder of this chapter.

Creating habits

Starting a habit to reduce burnout and increase balance requires thoughtful planning.

You may be thinking, *Change is hard! What if I fail? I prefer my comfort zone.* I've felt that way, too. But if you start small, you can create a new comfort zone. **If you incorporate one tiny new habit into your routine, one that takes three minutes or less, you won't feel like you're making a huge, radical change.** Then, your comfort zone will include this new healthier habit.

Change can be intimidating, mostly because it brings uncertainty. Many people prefer the familiarity of their current situation, even if it's not ideal, over the discomfort of the unfamiliar. Many people "stick with the devil they know versus the angel they don't." Change and growth often require being uncomfortable. This is true for any new endeavor.

One example of this was when I trained for triathlons. Muscle aches reminded me that I was pushing my body in new ways and that temporary discomfort was a sign of progress. The same applies to developing new habits in your professional life.

You might be worried about how your boss, colleagues, or team will react to your new habit. If you decide to take a short walk every day during lunch, your coworkers might ask, *"Where are you going? Why are you leaving? You are doing this every day?"* You might have to say, *"I'm taking a quick break to get some air and clear my mind for a few minutes,"* or *"I'm going to walk around the block during my lunch break going forward—I found that when I do this, I come back to work refreshed and energized."*

It might feel uncomfortable at first to set that boundary. But remember, you're not excluding anybody or doing anything wrong—you're actually doing the opposite by setting an example of self-care. By consistently taking that break, you'll return to work more refreshed and focused, which benefits everyone. Soon, your colleagues will likely respect your routine, and it might even inspire them to adopt healthier habits, too.

Here's everything you need to know about creating a new habit so you're set up for success and feel confident that you can make it stick.

Commit to achieving small goals

When starting a new habit your goal should be so small that it feels too simple to mention or even embarrassing to say out loud.

"I'm going to read a single email from a professional newsletter each day."

"I'm going to organize one file on my desktop before leaving the office."

Make the goal so small that you have no excuse not to do it. This approach ensures you'll feel confident in completing the task without it feeling impossible or overwhelming.

You and I both know you can easily commit and follow through on spending two minutes reading a newsletter or organizing a single file and if you do more than your commitment, GREAT!

These *micro-habits* will:

1. Help you stick to a new routine
2. Make a big difference over time.

When you're first developing a habit, the focus should be on the consistency of the act itself, not the time spent. If your goal is "easy," you're more likely to do it. Create a sustainable habit you can maintain for lasting balance, not just a one-time effort that can't be maintained over time.

As you continue with your micro-habit, you'll notice a couple of things will start to happen.

First, it will become second nature—organizing that file or reading the newsletter will no longer feel like an effort.

Second, you'll naturally start to do more. That one minute might turn into five, and before you know it, you'll be building on that small habit naturally.

Third, you will see progress and consistency toward your goal.

Do one thing at a time

Both at work and home, we often take on more than we can comfortably manage. When it comes to building habits, less is more. **To successfully implement any new habit, focus on one at a time.**

By mastering and fully integrating one habit into your routine before moving on to the next, you set yourself up for success, ensuring the longevity of each habit you begin.

A new habit starts with the first small step. Back to the desktop organization example, if you want to start a habit of organizing your desktop files, the first step might be creating folders for how you want to have your files organized. Don't *also* start organizing other areas of your computer until after you have the desktop completed.

If you want to start drinking more water throughout the day, pick one time or one place where you'll drink more water. This could look like taking a sip every time you log into your computer or keeping a bottle next to your bed to drink before going to sleep.

Once you have one new habit in place, then add another. It may seem silly and super micro-managing to strictly do only one at a time, but research proves this is the successful way of making habits stick and sustainable.[21]

Create a ritual surrounding your habit

Create a ritual before the act of the habit you're trying to cultivate. When practiced consistently, your ritual will create momentum leading into the habit. Adding a post-habit ritual that feels like a reward will further reinforce the habit.

For example, when I was writing this and my prior book, the only consistent time I had to focus was in the early morning before getting the kids ready for school. To get my mind and body in the spirit of writing, I built a ritual to prepare for writing time. I'd get dressed (staying in my PJs did not help get into writing mode) and ready for the day, make a pot of coffee, prep lemon-infused water, and spray essential oils around my laptop. Doing this every time before I sat down to write signaled my mind and body that it was time to focus.

Once my writing time was up, and the morning routine with the kids was about to begin, I'd finish my coffee, close my laptop, and take a minute to breathe deeply. The ritual of drinking lemon water afterward became a refreshing reward.

Your post-habit ritual should be rewarding and give you an immediate feeling of accomplishment. It could be a delicious protein smoothie after a workout, a delightful 5-minute break to watch a funny video after a focused work block, or, if you're like me, the satisfaction of marking an X on the calendar for each day that you completed your new habit. If this appeals to you, *download the habit tracker tool that I created for you:*

Create rhythm and routine

Creating a rhythm and routine will help you be accountable for your habits and safeguard them from sabotage. Here's how.

Incorporate your new habit plans into your calendar. Having time dedicated in your calendar for your new habit is a step closer to ensuring that time is protected and it's a constant reminder every time you look at your schedule. See the Efficiency chapter for more on this. I inserted "walk break" at 1:50 p.m. every day for 10 minutes on my work calendar.

Create a consistent routine and stick to it. Just like the concept of building a ritual to create and nurture a new habit, our bodies are creatures of routine. The best way to start and keep a habit is to do it at the same time every day. The body gets hungry or has cravings at the same time every day, and creating a good habit works the same way. Be consistent and get it going like clockwork.

Try to never miss a habit twice in a row. This will keep you on track and you won't lose the habit before it starts. You don't want NOT doing the habit to become a habit.

Make your new habit obvious

Create cues in your environment to remind you to do your habit. Put your water bottle next to your keys so you remember to take it when you leave the house. Place your book on your bed opened to the page you're on so you have no choice but to pick it up before you get into bed.

Make your new habit attractive

Whatever new habit you're trying to create, make it visually appealing. Keeping with the desktop example, you could color-coordinate the folders. When I started the habit of drinking more water, I bought myself an insulated bottle that I love looking at and wanted to bring with me everywhere. If you want to take more notes in meetings, get a notebook that you enjoy looking at and a pen that you enjoy writing with.

Remove all habit barriers

When starting a new habit, remove all potential barriers and distractions that could get between you and your habit. You may not know what all the barriers are until after you begin, but in the meantime, try to imagine the before, during, and after of your habit and what you'll need to be successful. Do all you can to eliminate any obstacles that could get in the way of achieving your new habit.

When I decided to make a habit of meditating every day, I found a meditation app on my phone and set the notification alarm to go off at my scheduled wake-up time. The first thing I did when I woke up was click the notification and go into the app. My obstacle was this: Many mornings my husband and potentially a child would be in bed with me—not a prime meditation environment with sleepers and snorers next to me. So I kept my earbuds close by so as not to disturb them. I didn't want anything to get in the way of my effort to meditate every morning. Now I have no excuse to skip meditation in the morning. I have my tiny goal of one minute, my app, and my earbuds.

Figure out your triggers and create a coupling strategy

Triggers and coupling can help prime your mind and body for activating and sustaining a habit. You can use triggers when building a new habit by creating associations and subconscious couplings between two things that you want to follow each other.

What exactly is a trigger? **Triggers are stimuli that prompt a specific emotional, cognitive, or physical response, and can be anything from something you see, hear, smell, feel, or even certain situations.** An example of this is the ping of our email notifications which is an audible trigger leading us to check our inbox after hearing that sometimes delightful, sometimes frustrating sound.

Coupling is the association between the trigger and the resulting behavior; it happens when a trigger (e.g., the time of day, environment, or emotional state) is paired repeatedly with a specific action (e.g., grabbing a snack, checking your phone, or responding with frustration).

The benefit of coupling is that your mind and body can associate an action with the trigger, creating a habit that you choose. It could be that you have a habit of going to the bathroom every time a meeting ends, or you always check your phone for messages when you sit down at your desk.

Coupling can also be used to recognize negative habits that you want to get rid of. For example, stress-eating is a common challenge many of my clients express to me. Here's why it's so difficult to break the habit of snacking when stressed: Feeling anxious or stressed is the trigger. The stress gets coupled with reaching for comfort food, which offers a quick rewarding feeling. And the next thing they know, they're reaching for the kids' Halloween stash whenever they feel stressed. In this scenario, stress and snacking have become linked, and snacking becomes a knee-jerk, instinctive reaction to stress, without conscious awareness or intentional thought.

Here's an example of how work stress is coupled with burnout. An employee may notice that every time they have a tight deadline (trigger), they sacrifice their self-care (not sleeping or eating well) to get the work completed (behavior). Multiple and consistent deadlines = burnout.

Understanding and recognizing coupling allows you to make a conscious effort to respond differently and change the associated behavior.

Here are some positive ways to use triggers and coupling:

- "Whenever I finish a meeting (trigger), I'll take a few minutes to summarize the key points and action items (behavior)."
- "Every time I receive a notification (trigger), I'll pause to take three deep breaths before responding (behavior)."
- "Whenever someone asks about my availability (trigger), I'll open my calendar to check and confirm (behavior)."
- "Whenever I feel stress coming on (trigger), I'll take a short walk before returning to the task at hand (behavior)."

By coupling these simple actions with specific triggers, you can create a more productive and intentional work routine that is supportive of your goals and natural flows.

Here are the types of triggers that can be used to build coupling associations:

Location. A location trigger is when a habit manifests around a specific physical place or condition, like checking the mailbox before opening your front door or opening the fridge every time you walk into the kitchen, even if you're not hungry.

For example, imagine you step into the office break room to grab a cup of coffee, but you find yourself reaching for a donut because they're always there. Soon enough, every time you go to the break room, whether it's for coffee or something else, you're also grabbing a donut. Location triggers often lead to automatic behaviors and mindless habits because your actions become subconscious responses to your environment. You most likely wouldn't have grabbed a donut if you weren't in the break room.

With some intentionality and adjusting to your environment, you can use location triggers in your favor to create healthy and productive habits.

Have you noticed that when you start a new job or move to a new office it's easier to start a new routine? That's because new habits are easier to start in new locations, where you don't have preconditioned triggers to overcome.

When I'm feeling drained and not particularly motivated to focus, getting myself into a dedicated workspace, like the library or a co-working space, can trigger my mind into productivity mode. By setting a small goal, like tackling one task for five minutes or responding to two emails, I'm able to kickstart my momentum. Of course, once I start, I often end up working longer because I'm already there and have gotten into a flow.

Time. Morning habits are one of the most common examples of time triggers. We all have a series of habits that we do after waking up in the morning or after starting the workday, such as getting coffee, checking emails, reviewing the day's schedule, or attending a morning stand-up meeting. There are also other time triggers throughout the day that are less obvious, like reaching for a midmorning snack, checking social media right after lunch, or reaching for a beer at the end of the day. Many time-triggered habits stem from our natural daily rhythms. When you understand why your habits happen at specific times every day, you can more easily reinforce a positive habit or introduce a new habit to replace an unproductive or unhealthy one.

One of my clients wanted to start a midday mental reset. After discussing her goals we set a daily alarm on her phone to go off at 2 p.m. with the reminder to "breathe." At that time, she would place all her devices on "do not disturb" and sit silently for three minutes, focusing on her breath. After a few weeks, she started instinctively checking the time to see how far away her 2 p.m. break was and noticed that she checked just minutes before 2 p.m. Her body was now accustomed to the new habit.

Events. The alarm in the example above is also an event-related habit trigger. You can start an event-triggered habit by associating your new behavior with a regular event. To increase focus and reduce stress, for example, you could take one deep breath every time your phone pings, instead of grabbing it instantly. Countless events happen throughout the day that are fantastic cues for leveraging habits, like closing your laptop and turning the car off. If you're trying to drink more water, start taking a sip of water every time you get into the car and/or every time you end a phone call. In a team environment, an example of this could be that at the beginning of every weekly team meeting everyone shares something they're grateful for or a favorite moment from the week. After a few times doing this, everyone will naturally come to the meeting prepared with their share, making the meeting the event-related trigger for the habit of remembering a happy moment or grateful thought.

Emotions. Emotions play a big role in habits and tend to be a trigger for bad habits. Feeling tired, bored, or lonely typically leads to habits of unnecessary snacking, unproductive multitasking, or disconnected scrolling through social media.

Managing emotions can be particularly challenging when trying to build new, positive habits. This is the hardest trigger to build a habit with as it involves intentionality and emotional awareness, which means observing and reflecting on your emotional states to understand how they influence your behaviors. Being aware of your emotions is powerful when creating and maintaining a balanced life, and should be a constant practice. Even as a person with a consistent practice of personal reflection and emotional awareness, I am constantly learning from my emotional states.

When I find myself stressed, I use that emotional trigger to practice calming techniques, like box breathing. Box breathing is where you breathe in for a count of four, hold your breath for a count of four, exhale for a count of four, and hold again for a count of four, then repeat the cycle. This simple technique helps to calm the nervous system and get the body back to a composed and regulated state. Try it the next time you find yourself in a stressful moment.

Pro tip: When choosing to use a trigger to build a habit, make sure it's specific and immediately actionable. *"I'll review my to-do list right after our daily stand-up meeting,"* or *"I'll drink a glass of water every time I finish a conference call."* Experiment with different triggers to see what works best for you.

Other people. Have you heard the saying by Jim Rohn that we are the average of the five people we spend the most time with? There's also the, *"Show me your friends, and I'll show you your future"* derivative. The intent of both is the same and the message is clear—who we spend time with influences our behaviors and mindset, which directly impacts who we are and who we will become. If your colleagues or work friends have healthy and productive habits and behaviors, you're more likely to adopt those. If they have strong work ethics and volunteer on the weekends, you're more likely to do those activities. Same goes if those around you regularly engage in counterproductive behaviors. If they go to happy hour and share a pitcher of beer and gossip about teammates after every work day, you'll most likely end up with a pint glass in your hands, engaging in the rumor mill many evenings.

One study in the New England Journal of Medicine found that if your friend becomes obese, then your risk of obesity increases by 57 percent—even if your friend lives hundreds of miles away.[22] If a close colleague becomes less engaged or demotivated, it can affect your levels of engagement and productivity. Wild, right?! The best way to make positive use of the "other people" trigger is to surround yourself with people who have the habits and attitudes you want to have.

Make the choice, every day

Before habits become ingrained, they are an active choice you have to make, every single day. When you make the choice and follow through, you'll feel empowered! And if nothing else goes right in your day, that one-to-three minutes you took to devote to your new habit will be something you can be proud of.

Quitting habits

Simply trying to quit a bad habit often isn't effective. Talk to anyone who's trying to stop smoking, drink less alcohol, or watch less TV, and they'll tell you how difficult it is to quit a bad habit. **The most successful approach to quitting an unwanted habit is to replace it with a more desirable one.** For example, if you want to stop drinking multiple cups of coffee throughout the day, try substituting a cup or two with a healthier alternative, like herbal tea or sparkling water. Or if you have a habit of scrolling social media after lunch, instead, take a 5-minute walk or do a quick stretch session. Not only will you break the cycle of mindless scrolling but you'll boost your energy and productivity for the rest of the day— efficiency and habits double win! If you want to watch less TV, set a time limit or activate the snooze function and replace some screen time with cooking a new recipe, going for a walk, or engaging in a hobby or creative project.

Avoid feeding the habit

Another way to break a bad habit is to take yourself away from the place and time it generally happens. For example, I used to experience an energy dip every afternoon around 2 p.m. which led to grabbing a sweet treat from my desk drawer. This became my go-to routine: As soon as the afternoon slump hit *(trigger)*, I'd reach for a stash of sweets—Rice Krispie treats, chocolate-covered almonds, and chocolate bars *(behavior)*. Despite trying to limit myself to a small handful of almonds or two squares of chocolate, I often ended up eating the whole thing (it's hard to resist when it's within arm's reach).

One day, I realized that this habit wasn't giving me the boost I wanted, and I decided to make a change. Instead of reaching for the treat drawer, I removed myself from my desk and went for a short walk.

To support this new habit, I stopped being near the bad habit culprit (the sweets drawer) at the habituated time. I set an alarm (event-trigger) and proactively began my walk at 1:50 p.m., *before* the craving set in, making it easier to avoid the magnetic pull to the drawer. That simple ten minutes made all the difference. I told a coworker what I was doing, and she helped hold me accountable. Sometimes she'd join me on the walk. And sometimes she simply reminded me of the time.

I also stopped "feeding" the old habit with a few changes, by stocking my drawer with nuts and jerky instead of treats. This sounds simple, but it was effective. After that, when I got a craving and reached inside the drawer, satiating protein and crunchy nuts were there to greet me. Sweet tooth curbed!

Within a month, my 2 p.m. sweets craving was eliminated, and in a double whammy of health, I got more steps in and my blood flowing as well. When I returned to my desk, my brain worked even better than before; I felt refreshed and more productive. By making small, intentional changes, I was able to replace a bad habit with a positive one, leading to better health and greater work performance.

Accountability and safeguarding (to make habits stick)

Accountability means being responsible for yourself and your habits. You cannot outsource your habit; it is yours to own.

Safeguarding **means taking measures to protect your habit and prevent it from being derailed.**

By telling my coworker what my intentions and goals were, she was able to help hold me accountable, but it was up to *me* to leave my desk and walk away.

Another way to hold yourself accountable is to focus on the desired outcome and not on the initial action. As we talked about at the beginning of this chapter, motivation, and inspiration wax and wane, which leads to not always feeling inspired to act on the habit you're trying to create and nurture. But when you focus on how it makes you feel *after* you've completed the action, you'll be more compelled to get to the desired outcome. You may not feel like you *want* to spend three minutes listening to a personal development book at a particular moment, but you can remind yourself how much you like the feeling of learning, growing, and accomplishment. You may not *want* to go to yoga first thing in the morning, but to help you get there, you can focus on how awesome it makes you feel after you do.

Slip vs slide

Of course, unexpected events inevitably happen and disrupt your routines. A sudden client meeting, urgent project deadline, or unexpected issue that requires your immediate attention—all of these can ruin your best-laid plans. Your midday walk might be foiled when you have to tend to a last-minute request by a client or boss. Or, an after-work networking event leaves you too tired to complete your usual end-of-day tasks, like organizing your desk or planning for the next day.

These are normal and natural "slips" in your good habit formation. What you want to avoid is allowing a slip to become a "slide."

You can pop back up quickly from a *slip*, but in a *slide*, you fly down a slippery slope for an unknown amount of time with less control.

The benefit of having a habit become part of your routine is you'll have a strong foundation to adjust and adapt as needed and bounce back quickly. Your new habit, when woven into your routine, will feel like something you can't go the day without doing. When your routine gets jolted, you'll probably not feel right without it and be eager to get back to it.

More ways to make a habit stick

Create a support network. When relevant and appropriate, share your new habits and goals with your colleagues, manager, etc. They can help keep you accountable and remind you of your commitment. When your team and peers understand your goals, they can support you and even help champion your success. You might even inspire someone to take on a new healthy habit too.

Make it meaningful. One of the most impactful ways to create lasting change is to attach the greatest meaning you can to it.

You aren't just doing this for yourself; think about how this change impacts the rest of your life and the people around you.

Chronic stress can lead to mental and physical health problems, including anxiety and depression, heart disease, and addiction. Shocking fact: Work-related stress is a direct factor in around 120,000 people's deaths every year.[23] With a more proactive approach, healthy habits can improve your productivity, create space for creativity, support achieving long-term goals, path to promotion, and create space for hobbies that bring you joy and provide feelings of balance.

Your role and presence highly affect the lives of those closest to you. Whether you think of yourself as a role model or not, you are, both inside and outside of work.

By creating and sustaining healthy habits that have meaning for you and enable you to have more balance in your life, you're showing those around you how to do the same. Your family, friends, and colleagues will see the positive impact of your efforts and, consciously or not, feel permission to do the same. When you assign deeper meaning to your new habit and align it with your deepest purpose in life, the more likely you'll stick with it.

Make your habit non-negotiable. Create enough importance around your new habit that you aren't willing to risk failure. When I was twenty-four, I worked in the Human Resources department at Juicy Couture while in graduate school getting my Masters Degree in Organizational Management. I guess that wasn't busy enough, because I decided to compete in a triathlon.

I had to figure out how to fit in triathlon training while working full-time and going to classes at night. I was already going directly from work to school most days, and then home, where I did homework and not much else before going to bed. *How would I make sure I fulfilled my commitment to myself?*

The first thing I did was to find a bigger reason than myself to do the race (see advice above). I discovered a group called Team in Training, which is a part of the Leukemia and Lymphoma Society. My grandmother passed away from leukemia and my grandfather had it at the time too, so it was a cause close to my heart. Team in Training provided a supportive environment with coaches, mentors, training plans, and a team of accountability partners to support my goal of crossing the finish line. And I would do it while simultaneously fundraising for the Leukemia and Lymphoma Society. This was perfect. After I told my grandfather what I was doing, there was no turning back. I had to figure out how to fit everything in and make it non-negotiable so I wouldn't allow myself to falter on my commitment.

I lived about fifteen miles from my office and decided to ride my bike to work. I figured that the 30-mile round-trip was perfect for my bike training during the week. The first morning, I woke up early, packed my work bag with baby wipes, deodorant, and baby powder so I wouldn't smell like a bomb of body odor at work, and lugged my bike out with all my best intentions. I plugged in my earbuds and cranked Metallica. "Take my hand, we're off to Never-Neverland!" Oh, yeah. I was strong. Powerful. Unstoppable.

Ten minutes into my ride, I was dripping with sweat and filled with regret. Many grunts, spits, laments, and tears later, I pulled up to work with jelly legs. I couldn't believe I'd have to repeat the ride when it was time to go home later! But, that was the point. I left myself no out. I had to ride my bike home. (There was no Uber or Lyft in those days.)

Even though I wanted to quit right then and there, the commitment I made to my grandfather and everyone who had donated to my fundraising campaign kept me going—I wasn't willing to give up and have to tell all those people that I had quit. Thankfully the ride home went much smoother, and I was proud of myself.

Common challenges and fears

When we consider making a change, especially in our habits, it's easy to get caught up in common challenges and fears. You might think, *"What if I fail? What if this doesn't work for me and is a waste of time? What if there's a different approach that would be better for me?"* These doubts can hold us back from even starting.

The fear of failure and the fear of the unknown can be paralyzing, but I'm here to remind you that every meaningful change involves *some* risk. Instead of going into a state of avoidance and paralysis, approach these fears with curiosity. Ask yourself, *"What's the worst that could happen?"* Often, the reality isn't nearly as scary as the fear itself.

And remember, progress is progress, no matter how small. The only true failure is staying stuck in the patterns that aren't serving you, especially when they're contributing to your burnout.

Overcoming fear by priming your mind

Giving yourself an inspirational speech and getting your head right before you take on something new are examples of priming your mind. Whether it's delivering a presentation, leading a meeting, or starting a new habit, priming your mind helps you approach these moments with confidence. Additionally, you can anticipate challenges and remind yourself of your strengths and capabilities.

When facing a task or new habit you're hesitant to start, remind yourself, *"I'm willing to be uncomfortable temporarily to get the results I'm looking for. It will be worth it. I have started new things in the past. I can do hard things!"* Once you get past the initial discomfort, you'll find your rhythm and reap the benefits of time and energy well spent.

Handling resistance

Our resistance to change is a complex beast. Some people see resistance as laziness or lacking willpower, but that's not usually the case. Often, it stems from a mix of psychological and practical barriers.

From a psychological perspective, our brains are wired to prioritize comfort and familiarity.[24] When we know what to expect, we feel safe, because we know what the outcome will be. Our current habits, whether they serve us or not, feel safe because they're predictable. Change, on the other hand, triggers uncertainty, and that uncertainty can feel like a threat, even if we know the change is for our benefit.

There are also practical barriers. We tell ourselves we *want* to change, but logistics get in the way. Exhaustion is real, and it could be the time commitment or the mental energy required to shift a habit that gets in the way of making a change. The idea of fitting something new into an already packed schedule feels overwhelming, so we don't even start. Or maybe we don't have the tools or the environment isn't set up to support the change. Again, the change doesn't need to be drastic to be effective. Remember the micro-habits we talked about before? Small, incremental shifts have a massive impact over time.

If you feel resistance creeping in, pause and ask yourself: *What's really holding me back? Is it fear of the unknown? Or maybe a practical hurdle that can be solved with a little planning?* Recognizing the real source of your resistance is the first step in overcoming it.

Take a close look at your day and pinpoint where you naturally resist change—maybe it's in the morning when you're groggy and default to old habits, or perhaps it's in the evening when you're too tired to try something new. Or maybe it's at work when you are surrounded by people who are all seemingly set in their ways.

Once you've identified these resistance points, address them by making small adjustments. For example, if you resist change because mornings are tough, try prepping the night before so your new habit feels less overwhelming when you wake up.

The ADKAR change management model

When managing personal change effectively, having a structured approach can make all the difference. One proven method is the ADKAR model, which stands for *Awareness, Desire, Knowledge, Ability, and Reinforcement.*[25]

First, you need to build **Awareness** of *why* the change is necessary.

Next, cultivate the **Desire** to make the change, connecting it to your personal goals and values.

Then, equip yourself with the **Knowledge** you need to succeed, by learning new skills or gaining deeper insight into the habit you want to form.

Ability follows, which is all about putting that knowledge into action, and practicing the new habit until it becomes second nature.

Finally, **Reinforcement** is key to ensuring the change sticks, by celebrating your progress, and finding ways to keep yourself motivated long-term.

Let's say you're struggling with time management (a huge stressor for many). Your days are chaotic, filled with back-to-back meetings and never-ending to-do lists. Here's how ADKAR can help you avoid burnout and create a new way to approach time management.

Awareness: Acknowledge the impact of poor time management on your productivity and stress levels, realizing that if you don't make a change, your work, health, and personal life will continue to suffer. This awareness makes it clear that something has to shift.

Desire: Connect the change to your personal goals of wanting to be more effective at work, have more time for your family, and reduce your stress. These desires give you the motivation to take action.

Knowledge: Seek information on effective time management techniques, read books, attend workshops, and even ask for advice from colleagues who excel in this area. Learn about prioritizing tasks, setting boundaries, and the importance of planning your day. (You are reading this book, so you are already on your way.)

Ability: Put these time management techniques into practice. Start small, setting aside 15 minutes each morning to plan your day and prioritize your tasks. Over time, you'll become more proficient at managing your schedule, and these new habits become a part of your daily routine.

Reinforcement: To ensure the changes stick, regularly review your progress and celebrate your wins, no matter how small— perhaps a sparkling cider cheers at dinner to acknowledge a day well-managed or a celebratory massage at the end of a week where you worked long hours to finish a project. Share your success with a mentor who has been providing ongoing encouragement. This reinforcement helps you maintain your new habits and continue improving your time management skills.

At-home habits influence workplace stress

Your habits at home play a powerful role in shaping your performance at work.

When you're intentional about building healthy habits outside of work—whether it's maintaining a regular exercise routine, getting enough sleep, spending time in nature, or setting aside time for reflection and relaxation—you set the stage for success in the workplace. Good habits at home create a foundation of discipline, resilience, and well-being that naturally carries over into your work.

When you start your day with a calm, centered morning routine, for example, that sense of groundedness and focus tends to follow you into the office. Likewise, when you make it a habit to manage stress effectively in your personal life, you're better equipped to handle the pressures of your job, and vice versa.

Habits don't exist in silos; they shape the character of who we are, influencing how we show up in every area of our lives. By committing to healthy and intentional habits at work or home, we're improving our lives in both places, and we're setting ourselves up for greater success and satisfaction in life overall.

How to choose, develop, and nurture a habit

Choosing a habit to start or stop

To figure out which habit you'd like to implement the most right now, start with a brain dump. Go ahead, get it all out, and make this list as big as you can! If you're having trouble thinking of habits to start, here's some food for thought: *Exercise every day • Plan for the week ahead • Keep workspace tidy and organized • Drink eight cups of water per day • Get eight hours of sleep per night • Meditate for five minutes per day • Prioritize tasks each morning • Do weekly task prioritization, meal planning and meal prepping • Use social media for no more than ten minutes per day • Do positive affirmations each morning*

1. Make a list of the habits you'd like to have, of any size.
2. Look at your list and circle the habit(s) that will help you create more ease and balance in your day-to-day life.
3. Of your circled habits, pick one that you can easily create a trigger for, like creating a phone alarm, or based on a location, like when walking into the kitchen or as soon as you arrive at your desk.
4. Next, write down the ONE big, broad habit you'd like to create.

5. Now, what is the smallest version of that habit that you're capable of completing every day?

6. Finally, write down the smallest and most doable goal and the trigger it's associated with to help you start forming your habit.

Fantastic! You've identified what habit to create (or stop!) and you've set a doable goal. You're on your way.

Making your habit stick

1. **Make your habit goal non-negotiable.** Don't make it a choice—make it impossible to do anything but the thing you've set out to do. The more "outs" you give yourself, the more you're setting yourself up for failure. Write down how you're going to create the conditions that will make your habit easy to do.

2. **Think about the routine that your new habit will be a part of.** What ritual will you do immediately before the habit? What are the triggers that you will associate with the habit? (Location, time, events, emotions, and other people.)

3. **Is your habit attractive, easy, obvious, and satisfying?** If you answered "no" to any part of this question, ask why and write down how you'll remove any barrier that gets in the way of making it attractive, easy, obvious, and satisfying.

4. **Who are the people in your life who should know about this habit?** Write down who the people are who can help hold you accountable.

Nurture your habit

1. **Reflect and write about the reasons why you want this habit.** What situations will it fix if you develop this new

habit? How does having this habit benefit your life and help you create balance?

2. **Think and write about the worst-case scenario if you acted on creating this new habit.** Chances are it's not a life-or-death consequence and it's 100 percent worth trying. If the worst-case scenario happens, ask yourself if you'd be able and willing to handle it.

3. **Make a list of all the ways that creating your new habit will benefit other areas of your life.**

Habits wrap-up

Your life is made up of thousands of small habits. To decrease burnout and stress, you must create habits that serve you and remove the ones that don't. Habits are foundational for sustaining productivity and maintaining balance, especially when motivation wanes from your original inspiration.

✓ **Habits aren't just for health.** They're for attention span and brain flow as well. When you're primed to be productive, getting tons done will be more efficient and less stressful.

✓ **Habits vs. motivation.** Habits are more reliable than motivation for sustained success; they become automatic actions that don't require conscious thought.

✓ **Micro-habits.** Start with small, manageable goals that can be done consistently to build momentum and avoid overwhelm. Try the "1 percent better" approach. Small incremental changes to an existing routine or habit can lead to significant progress over time. Instead of starting an entirely new habit, focus on enhancing something you're already doing. A one percent change is better than doing nothing.

✓ **Triggers and coupling.** Use triggers, like specific times, locations, or events, to naturally activate a habit. Coupling habits with other actions helps reinforce them.

✓ **Accountability and sustainability.** Share your goals with others for support and use systems like habit trackers to safeguard your progress. Your success means you're setting a great example for others. (I go over communication best practices in the next chapter.)

✓ **Overcoming resistance.** Resistance to change is normal (familiar = safe) but can be tackled through small, consistent actions that gradually lead to lasting habit formation. Overcoming resistance to change starts with understanding (and accepting) that temporary discomfort can be part of the process.

Building healthy and productive habits isn't always easy, but I hope these tools help you make lasting changes. It takes intentional effort and consistency to turn an act into a habit. You have all you need to create habits to support your health, goals, balance, and overall well-being. Ready to share your new habit goal(s) with your community? The next chapter on Communication will share how.

Communication

Clarity and comprehension skills for achieving balance

"The single biggest problem in communication is the illusion that it has taken place."

— *George Bernard Shaw*

You probably feel like all you do all day is communicate, whether you're leading meetings, writing emails and reports, messaging with colleagues, providing feedback on projects, talking to clients, discussing plans, asking for or giving advice, or fielding yet another scam call.

You may talk or write a lot, but are you truly communicating? Are you being misunderstood? Do you feel like you need to repeat yourself a lot? Are things not going smoothly even though you feel you've made your expectations and plans clear? Do you feel like you have to explain yourself over and over?

Whether it's what you're saying or how others are hearing you, you can save a lot of time and frustration (and reduce burning out by repeating yourself over and over) by refining your communication skills.

Even the best communicators can learn and grow in this area because communication is not a static skill—it's dynamic and ever-evolving. As new generations enter the workforce, with the constant introduction of new technologies, and time being as limited as ever to get your point across, being clear and intentional about what you say and what you *hear* has never been more critical.

Communication and burnout

We've all been in a meeting, conversation, project, or team where communication has broken down; it's not pretty. Office resentments, bickering, "He said/she said/they said" problems, projects getting done incorrectly, and more can be a result of a single poorly written or expressed message.

When done right, communication can reduce disagreements, lower stress levels, bring teams together and get tasks done more quickly, creating more space for, you guessed it, balance.

Successful communication will reduce burnout by:

Decreasing misunderstandings. When the person or people you're communicating to understand the *why* behind what you're requesting or saying, it can cut down on unnecessary conflict. For example, if you're restructuring your day and canceling meetings to be more productive or asking your team to shift gears on a project, sharing your reasoning helps them understand your intentions and decisions. This also works for personal communication. Perhaps you need to skip a weekly dinner at your mother-in-law's house to finish a PowerPoint you're presenting the next day. By telling your partner *why* you need to refocus that time, they still may not be happy with your absence, but they won't be able to say they don't know why you aren't there.

When you share the intention behind your choices, you give others the context they need to understand and support you, even if they don't fully agree.

Lower stress levels. Two big contributors to stress are confusion and incorrect expectations. Being open cuts down on both. When you're open about your workload, priorities, and intentions, others are more likely to respect your boundaries and offer support, instead of piling more on you, pushing you closer to burnout. If they don't know what you need, they can't adapt to you and help.

Improve efficiency. When direction and purpose are clearly communicated, everyone around you will operate better, and ask fewer (or more strategic) questions. This will naturally lead to fewer distractions and more productivity. It's like giving everyone around you a roadmap. They know exactly where you're headed and why, which means they can operate more effectively without constantly needing to check in or ask for clarity.

Responding vs. reacting in communication

When was the last time a knee-jerk verbal or written reaction served you well in the long-run? Has a frustrated text in the middle of the night ever led to a positive result? Or has yelling back at a customer ever turned things around? In my experience, those approaches backfire 100% of the time.

Reacting quickly without thinking often leads to unnecessary stress and a poor outcome. But, when you take a moment to collect yourself before responding, you can calm your mind, and from that calmer place, you can respond more thoughtfully and intentionally, leading to a more constructive outcome. Giving yourself time (even just 10 seconds) before communicating can make all the difference.

Imagine your boss sent you an email about a recent report you did, and it's filled with an overwhelming amount of criticism. Instead of immediately replying with, "But I did exactly what you asked me to do!," take a breath, look at the feedback again from a lens of positive intention, and craft a more thoughtful response. In this space, you can write back something like, "Thank you for the email. I'd love to schedule a time to discuss your feedback and better understand your expectations before editing the report." Even though you may still be fuming with rage, your response doesn't need to reflect that.

Being proactive vs. reactive

When you know you're going to need support, give as much notice as possible to those you'll need help from. The help you need could be direct, such as asking someone to pitch in on a project, or indirect, like extending grace and understanding if you're not as responsive to emails as usual.

Communicate with your team and boss what specific help you may need, and (as mentioned above) *why* you need that help. The "why" is important so the other person can feel empathy toward your situation and be even more motivated to help. Respect their needs as well—ask whether they can do it and what they need to make sure that all goes smoothly.

It's a lot easier to get support *before* versus *during* the need. For example, if you know you'll be on vacation and a client will need a deliverable, bring your colleague or team in for support with as much lead time as possible rather than firing off a panicked email to them the night before you leave.

This strategy works well in your personal life as well. For example, if you need help with your usual after-dinner family to-do list, express to your partner, "Hey [insert pet name], I have a lot to do tonight. I have dozens of emails to respond to and a budget presentation to finish. There's also laundry to be folded and kids' lunches to be made. What are your plans after dinner? Would you be able to help clean up after dinner and fold the laundry? That would be a huge support to me, so I don't need to go to bed so late." Describing your needs in this way will work a lot better than if, after dinner, you say in a mid-martyr meltdown whilst slamming cabinets passive-aggressively, "Ugh, I have soooo much to do! I feel like I have to do *everything* around here!" and expect your (also tired) partner to know what to do and jump in at the last minute.

If your partner or roommate is the one slamming cabinets passive-aggressively, you can say "Hey [insert pet name], I'm noticing that you have a lot on your mind. Is there anything I can do to support you? I have a few emails to get through tonight, but I have space to take care of other tasks. Is there anything I can take off your plate?"

Being proactive versus reactive isn't just for the sake of others; it's for your sanity, too. Knowing you'll have the support you need ahead of time will increase your balance and reduce your burnout.

The art of simplicity in communication

In a world where we're constantly bombarded with information, keeping your messages concise and to the point isn't just about saving time—it's about preventing information overload and reducing decision fatigue, both of which are major contributors to unnecessary stress and burnout.

Think about how often you feel overwhelmed by a long and winding email or meetings when everyone is talking in circles, with no clear decision to be made. It's exhausting.

Here's how to simplify, so you can get your message heard and hopefully others will see the benefit and will communicate more simply as well:

1. **Before you send a message, ask yourself,** "*If a person reads this, what's the <u>one thing</u> I want them to know, feel, or take away from this message? What's the core point I need to convey?*" Stick to that. Use friendly but clear, straightforward language.
2. **If you have multiple points to share, format your message** by spacing ideas with bullet points or numbers.
3. **In the subject line of an email, or the first line of your message, headline the intent of the message,** whether it's an action needed, a feedback request, or a review. Adding this information to the subject line (with a date) can make it easier for the recipient to know if they need to open or respond right away and what mindset to approach the email with.

4. **If there are more than three points to convey, pick up the phone or schedule a meeting.** Most of the time, a meeting will be quicker than trying to jump between so many points in an email or direct message (DM).

5. **If there are any items to convey that could be emotion-producing,** such as if you're adding a large project to someone's bursting to-do list and anticipate them feeling overwhelmed, or if you're sharing a vulnerable idea with your boss, consider having a conversation versus written communication about it.

Sometimes it can (ironically) feel like it takes longer to craft a shorter message, but when you get the hang of it you'll notice a decrease in your stress and an increase in mental bandwidth as well.

More strategies for concise communication:

1. **Know your audience:** Focus on what's relevant for your audience. Ask yourself, *"What do they really need to know?"*

2. **Clarify your intent:** Before you start communicating, be clear about your purpose. Are you *informing or requesting*? Knowing your intent helps you stay on track and avoid going off on tangents.

3. **Use simple language:** You're not trying to win a vocabulary contest. Avoid jargon, complex language, or overly technical terms unless absolutely necessary. The goal is to make your message as accessible as possible.

4. **Be direct:** Get to the point quickly. This ensures that your message isn't buried under less important information. You can even add emojis where appropriate to convey tone without needing to add more words.

5. **Limit the scope:** We've all sent too much information to someone, either professionally or personally, and they (frustratingly) answer one of the items but not others. To avoid this, focus on one topic or decision at a time.

6. **Ask for feedback:** Especially in a verbal conversation, it's helpful to ask for feedback. A simple *"Did I miss anything?", "Does that make sense?"* or *"Any questions?"* provides an opportunity to clarify any points that may still be unclear.

Example messages:

In this email, you can see I added my intent and ask in the subject line. And I've outlined the email for ease on the eyes and the brain. And you'll see how I edited down even further for a direct message to be easier for my recipient to get to the core of the request.

Email:

Subject: Request for XYZ Project Update by September 5th

Hi Kyle,

I hope you're doing well!

I'm following up on the status of the XYZ project. Could you please provide me with a **brief update on the progress** by the end of the day on **Thursday, September 5th**? Specifically, I'm looking for information on the following:

1. **Current progress:** Are we on track to meet the September 15th deadline?
2. **Any obstacles:** Are there any issues or delays that we need to address?
3. **Next steps:** What are the immediate next steps planned for this week?

This update will help us ensure that we're aligned and ready to present our findings to the leadership team next week.

If there's anything you need from my side to move forward, please don't hesitate to ask.

Thanks so much for your attention to this!

Jenna

Direct message:

> Hi Kyle. Quick check-in on the XYZ project—please **send me a brief update by EOD Thursday, September 5th**? Specifically:
>
> 1. **Current progress**: Are we on track for the September 15th deadline?
> 2. **Any obstacles**: Any issues or delays that need addressing?
> 3. **Next steps**: What's planned for this week?
>
> I need this info to prepare for our leadership update next week. Let me know if you need anything from me. Thank you!

Meetings (making the most of your time together)

Meetings don't have to be dreaded, boring, unproductive, time sucks. A well-run meeting can not only be a, dare I say it, fun experience, but they're also a crucial piece of the puzzle for preventing burnout for you and your team.

Good meetings:

1. Create space for open communication, aligning on priorities, and addressing issues before they become stressors.
2. Help prevent the buildup of misunderstandings or unresolved problems that can lead to overwhelm.
3. Make it easier for you and the entire team to stay focused and motivated.
4. Give you or your boss a chance to ensure you have the resources you need.
5. Keep expectations managed and offer a chance for delegating, which supports you and your team's well-being.
6. A great chance to bond with your teammates.

That said, not all meetings are created equal, and not all meetings are necessary. Gathering for a team meeting just for the sake of it isn't good for anyone. Time is precious, and to support your balance, know when to cancel a meeting to allow that time to be repurposed for something more productive and meaningful.

Meeting tips

Here are some best practices for using your meeting time effectively and efficiently.

Know when to meet. If the information you're planning to give or seeking to get could be easily exchanged in an email or internal message, cancel the meeting. A meeting is for when you want live back and forth, or an exchange of ideas.

Before a meeting:

1. **Prepare an agenda:** Outline the topics you want to discuss. Share the agenda with your boss, direct reports, or team members in advance. If the agenda is sparse, it might make sense to give everyone their time back.
2. **Review progress:** Review any notes or action items from previous meetings. This will help you track progress and identify any ongoing challenges that need attention.
3. **Gather data:** Gather any relevant data or reports that support your discussion points. Having this information ready will help everyone make informed decisions.
4. **Confirm roles and responsibilities**: Decide who will be in charge of timing, keeping to the agenda, meeting notes, or if everyone will take notes for themselves. If your meeting is virtual, utilize an AI or other tool to record your meetings that will also process the recording, create a summary and tasks list.

During the meeting:

1. **Start with a check-in:** Begin meetings with a brief, friendly, personal check-in. This could be as simple as asking how

everyone is doing or a quick update on how things in their lives are going. Bonus points if you follow up on something they shared in your last meeting. Share first to break the ice for everyone else. Sharing (what you're comfortable with) allows you and everyone else to know what's going on with each other. You'll know if someone's family member just passed away or if kids are about to be on a holiday break, and the impact this has on your colleague.

2. **Follow the agenda:** Stick to the agenda to ensure all important topics are covered. Make sure everyone has the opportunity to contribute.

3. **Encourage open communication:** Foster a safe environment for thought-sharing. Ask open-ended questions and actively listen to everyone.

4. **Assign action items:** Clearly define action items, who is responsible for them, and set deadlines. This keeps everyone accountable and ensures progress is made.

5. **Summarize key takeaways:** Before ending the meeting, summarize the key decisions made, action items assigned, and any next steps. This helps reinforce what was discussed and ensures everyone is on the same page.

After the meeting:

1. **Send meeting notes:** Shortly after the meeting, send out a summary of the discussion, including key takeaways, action items, and deadlines. This serves as a reference for everyone and helps keep the momentum going.

2. **Follow up on action items:** Keep track of the action items and follow up as needed. If a task isn't progressing as planned, address it sooner rather than later to prevent issues from escalating.

3. **Reflect on the meeting:** Take a moment to reflect on the effectiveness of the meeting. Did you achieve your

objectives? Was the meeting productive? Consider what worked well and what could be improved for next time.

Stay connected between meetings: Keep the lines of communication open between meetings. Regular check-ins, even informal ones, help maintain alignment and support ongoing collaboration. And if you're ever stuck on, "Should I text this or call," the answer is probably call.

Understanding communication styles

As you know, there are as many communication styles as there are people. Everyone has their "way with words." Some are so short it can come across as cold. Others spend a long time explaining. Some like to infuse personal anecdotes into each communication, and some like to keep a more formal impersonal tone.

"I didn't mean *that*!"

A misread text is a problem as common as the barista spelling your name wrong on your coffee cup at Starbucks. It's so easy for messages to be misinterpreted. What you intended as a lighthearted or quick comment can come across as harsh or aggressive. My teenagers always think I'm mad at them when I text them "k." I'm not angry, I'm just responding quickly.

To mitigate these risks, take a moment to read over your message before sending it as if you are the person getting it. If the topic is sensitive or complex, consider picking up the phone or scheduling a quick video chat instead.

Three styles of communication

There are three styles that show up commonly in the workplace: Passive, aggressive, and assertive. Each style can impact our ability to maintain balance, especially when we're juggling myriad responsibilities at work and at home.

Passive communication

Passive communication is when we don't speak up for ourselves, often because we're avoiding conflict or don't want to burden others. It looks like saying "yes" when you really want to say "no" or staying silent when something is bothering you.

Example: You're asked to take on a project, but you're already maxed out. Instead of saying, *"I don't have the bandwidth for this right now,"* you say, *"Sure, I can handle it,"* and you secretly seethe at your increased workload.

The problem with being too passive: Over time, holding in what you really need and want builds resentment and frustration. If you're constantly putting others' needs before your own, without communicating your own, you're going to feel it—emotionally and physically.

To shift away from passive communication:

- **Use "I" statements, like "*I need...*" or "*I feel...,*" to share what your needs and opinions are.** You can't assume that others know or can guess your needs if you don't speak up. *"I need to extend the deadline on the marketing proposal. I feel that the current timeline doesn't give enough time for proper research, and I want to make sure that the proposal is thorough and not rushed."*
- **Practice setting boundaries.** Don't deny your inner gut or thoughtful reasoning and say yes only to people please. Chances are, it won't go well to say yes to requests and tasks you don't have the capacity for. Offer alternative solutions with your "no." If your boss asks you to do something urgent while you are already on a deadline for another assignment, you can respond by saying, *"I don't*

have the capacity to add this to my plate right now because I have XYZ due tomorrow. If you want to extend the deadline on XYZ, I can take this on. Or, *Colleen is really good at this also. She might be able to do it urgently."*

- **Be proactive.** Rehearse your response ahead of time making it easier to communicate your needs directly when the time is right.

Aggressive communication

Aggressive communication is when people bulldoze over others to get what they want. Communication like this comes across as demanding instead of asking, harsh in tone, or dismissive of others' ideas and feelings. While aggressive communicators may get what they want in the short term, it's damaging in the long run.

Example: Instead of saying, *"We need to adjust the timeline to meet our goals,"* an aggressive communicator might say, *"This is taking too long, and I need this done NOW."* The tone creates unnecessary stress and makes others feel like they need to walk on eggshells.

The problem with being too aggressive: Continuous aggressive communication creates tension and stress in relationships of all kinds, which adds even more pressure to our already full plates. Plus, no one wants to work with someone who's always pushing their agenda without consideration for everyone else.

If this is you, think about this cliche, which, as is often the case with cliches, is true: *"You can attract more bees with honey than vinegar"* before your next request or information share.

Assertive communication

Assertive communication is clearly stating your needs, feelings, and boundaries while respecting others. You're not shying away from difficult conversations, but you're not steamrolling anyone either. When you're assertive, you're able to respectfully say "no" and give your reason or an alternate solution when needed, delegate tasks, and speak up when something's not working.

Example: You're asked to take on a project, but you're at capacity. An assertive response would sound like, *"I'd love to help, but I have a full plate right now. If this can wait until next week, I'll be happy to take it on then. Otherwise, we'll need to reprioritize my other tasks or another solution."* It's clear, it's respectful, and it keeps you from taking on more than you can handle.

This method of communication prevents the buildup of frustration that can lead to mental and emotional exhaustion.

Examples of assertive communication

Here are more examples of integrating more assertiveness into your daily communication.

Clarity

Instead of *"When you have a minute, could you maybe send me an update?"*, go with *"Can you send me the project update by 3 p.m. tomorrow?"* You'll avoid any ambiguity and keep things moving forward.

Confidence without aggression

Instead of *"You need to get the new guy, Tom, up to speed ASAP,"* try, *"Tom just joined our project team. Since you know the project better than anyone, I'd appreciate if you could fill him in, so he can hit the ground running."* This keeps everyone in alignment with priorities and focused without putting anyone on the defensive.

Respect

"I know you've got a lot going on, but we'll need your feedback by Thursday to stay on track. Can you make that happen?" This approach shows you're mindful of someone else's situation while

still holding firm on what needs to be done. If relevant, you could also add, *"Is there anything that could potentially get in the way of getting your feedback by Thursday, or anything that I (or another teammate) can do to support you meeting this deadline?"*

Ownership of feelings

Instead of *"You're always ignoring my suggestions,"* try, *"I feel like my input isn't being considered, and I'd love to discuss how we can work through that."*

Listening

After making an ask, say *"What are your thoughts on this?"* This shows you're willing to hear the other person's side and collaborate.

Setting boundaries

Try saying, *"I can't take this on right now, but I'll be available next week to dive in."* You're setting a boundary but also offering a solution.

Tone

In emails or messages, be professional and friendly—no need for Harvard vocabulary, excessive punctuation or overly casual language. Instead of *"Yo Derek!!! 'Sup dude. I got a question for ya,"* try *"Hey Derek, hope all is well! I have a question for you regarding the XYZ project. Let me know a few times that work for you to connect this week."*

Navigating the fear of conflict

Some of the biggest hurdles people have when attempting clear communication is the fear of conflict, how others will react, or we don't want to be seen as difficult or uncooperative. But avoiding conflict doesn't make it go away. In fact, it usually makes a conflict worse. You can overcome the fear of conflict with a few strategies that make assertive communication, especially if this is new for you, feel less intimidating:

Shift your mindset

Instead of seeing assertive communication as a confrontation, think of it as a conversation. You're not picking a fight; you're simply advocating for yourself. People also often don't know the whole story, and think that things are worse or better than they actually are. Not only do most people appreciate clarity, but also by speaking up, you make it easier for everyone.

Practice in low-stakes situations

You don't have to dive into a high-pressure conversation right away. Practice being assertive in low-stakes situations, like requesting a change in a meeting time. As you get comfortable with these smaller asks, it'll be easier to tackle the bigger conversations.

Prepare yourself

If a potential conversation is making you anxious, it's okay to plan ahead. Think about what you want to say and how you want to say it. Write it down or role-play with somebody. The goal isn't to rehearse a script but to feel more confident going into the conversation. When you know your point and your reasons, it's easier to stay calm and focused.

Breathe through the discomfort

Assertive communication can be uncomfortable, especially if you're not used to it. But discomfort doesn't mean you're doing something wrong. When you feel anxiety rising, take a breath and ground yourself. Remind yourself that you were hired for your mind and skills, have the right to communicate your needs and ideas, and it's okay if it feels a little awkward at first. The discomfort is temporary and will probably pass after the conversation is over. Think of it as short-term discomfort for long-term gains of balance, for you and the person you're speaking with. With time and practice, it'll get easier.

Let go of excessive guilt

Guilt can be a powerful feeling to help us make moral and good decisions, but too much of it, whether placed on yourself or someone else, can lead to shame, which is counter-productive and can make or break situations and relationships.

Repeat this to yourself as needed:

I am not responsible for other people's feelings when I'm being respectful and clear about my needs. If someone reacts poorly to my boundary, that's on them—not me.

For example: Let's say you've been coming in early and staying late at work every day, feeling the pressure to put in extra hours to prove you're committed. You want to work more "normal" hours but are afraid you'll be seen as less dedicated or replaced by someone willing to burn the midnight oil who's been eyeing your position. Maybe you're also worried about your annual review coming up soon. This is a common fear in high-performing environments, where company culture often glorifies overworking. But as we know, working extra hours isn't always a sign of effectiveness or value. In fact, it often leads to burnout, which hurts performance in the long run.

When looking at overall performance, would you rather be seen as someone who pushes themselves too hard and burns out regularly, or, shows up and performs well consistently?

I personally want an employee who knows their limits and can be a consistent performer instead of someone who fluctuates in their ability to perform due to lack of self-awareness, self-care and healthy boundaries.

Let's say you're in this situation and want to stand up for yourself, but the fear of being replaced or undervalued is holding you back. Here's how you might approach the conversation:

You: *"Hi [Manager's Name], I'd like to talk to you about my workload and the hours I've been putting in recently. I've been coming early and staying late to keep up with everything, and I've noticed it's starting to impact my focus, attention to detail, and creativity. I want to make sure I'm delivering high-quality work and being as efficient and effective as possible during the day. I'd like to discuss work prioritization and/or potentially adjusting my workload so I can be as productive and successful as possible while having a more regular work schedule."*

In this conversation, you're not apologizing for needing balance, and you're not suggesting you're unwilling to work hard. You're being clear about your boundaries and framing the conversation around maintaining high-quality performance—something any good manager should respect. You're also opening up the opportunity to collaborate on solutions.

Handling difficult conversations

Needing to have a difficult conversation can be as stressful as a presentation to 1,000 people or approaching your opponent's line of hotels on a Monopoly game board when you already mortgaged half of your properties. (Seeing those red buildings always gets my heart racing.)

You might lose sleep for days before having a hard conversation—whether it be work-related or in your personal life. Maybe you have to let someone go from your team, need to discuss a change you want your partner to make in your relationship, or deliver bad news. You might be worried about how the person will react, what consequences will happen, if there will be anger, tears, or worst of all, no resolution at all.

Avoiding hard talks, while tempting, tend to make the situation worse. But by preparing yourself mentally and emotionally, you can walk into that conversation feeling grounded and confident.

Preparing for tough talks

Define your goal

Before you begin the conversation, get clear on what you want the outcome to be. Are you trying to solve a problem, set a boundary, or give feedback? Knowing your goal will help you stay focused if things get uncomfortable or emotional. Ask yourself, *"What's my ideal outcome here, and how can I guide the conversation toward that?"*

Every time I have to let someone go (the least favorite part of my job in HR), I prepare by picturing how I want the conversation to go and how I want the soon-to-be-ex-employee to feel coming out of the conversation. My goal is to always share something positive about their time at the company, be clear on the why of their termination, what the immediate next steps are, and ensure they know there is a follow-up in writing because once someone hears that they no longer have their job, they typically don't retain much information after that.

Manage your emotions

You may be more worried about the other person's emotions but don't neglect thinking about *your* emotional state. Emotions can run high in tough conversations, sometimes unexpectedly so, and it's easy to get swept up in them.

To avoid this, do some prep work before the conversation. Take a few deep breaths, talk with someone, role-play, or even journal about it. This will help you anticipate potential feelings that could arise during the conversation and process feelings of anxiety, frustration, or fear. If you feel the rise of emotions during the conversation, take a deep breath and remember what your goals are.

Another example where I needed to calm myself before having a constructive conversation, keeping with the theme of terminations, was when I had to let a teacher go from my preschool. I knew this was going to be tough because she was employed before I became her boss and she deeply cared about the students. But she also consistently didn't follow the rules and regulations that were both in the employee handbook and a part of the licensing protocols for a childcare facility. When I found out that she was keeping flaming-hot Cheetos and pistachios stashed in the classroom in a place easy for 2-year-olds to grab and potentially choke on, I just about lost my mind. I was flaming a lot hotter than her Cheetos when I found them. Not only were these choking hazards, but this was her 3rd offense. Before approaching her for the 3rd and final time, I practiced talking through the scenario and termination conversation with my business partner. By doing this, I was able to approach her with a calm demeanor and clear facts, and not allow my frustration and anger to guide the conversation.

If you're mid-conversation and emotions are running higher than is conducive to a productive conversation, assess if this is a scenario where you can ask to postpone the continuation of the conversation until after you (and/or others) have cooled off. I did this during a PIP (Performance Improvement Plan) conversation. I was sitting in with an employee and his manager when both of them got heated. The employee pushed back on the feedback, feeling his performance didn't warrant a PIP, and the manager aggressively retorted with his reasons for implementing the PIP. Emotions were rising above comfort levels, and since the main points had been delivered, I stepped in to offer that the conversation be paused here and we could all connect again about further details and next steps in a couple of days. This worked out in everyone's favor as the employee came to the follow-up conversation having had time to process and the manager was more grounded as well.

Anticipate the other person's perspective

Put yourself in the other person's shoes for a minute. *What do you think they'll likely feel or think? What might their concerns be?* By anticipating their perspective, you can prepare for how they might react and can then respond more thoughtfully.

Additionally, you can reverse the roles. Imagine you're on the receiving end of this conversation. *How would you want the person to handle it?*

Before my difficult conversation with the "choking hazards" teacher above, I anticipated that she was going to be highly emotional, combative, and uncooperative. I thought about how I would want to be talked to if the roles were reversed. I discovered that if I was in her shoes, I'd potentially feel like this was unfair considering how much dedication she had given to the school over the years. With this in mind, I approached the conversation from a place of compassion, while also making sure the conversation was direct, and to the point, and didn't allow space for rebuttal.

Go to "The Balcony"

In addition to putting yourself in their shoes, try to put yourself in the position of being a fly on the wall or standing on a balcony above the scenario. When you remove yourself from the situation, and look at it objectively "from above" as though it were happening to someone else, you can gain a lot of perspective on what you'd like to see (or avoid) in the interaction. Think about what would make you the most proud of after leaving the conversation.

Plan, but stay flexible

It's smart to have a plan or some notes for what you want to say, but be careful not to script things out too rigidly. Conversations have a way of taking unexpected turns, and if you're too focused on sticking to a script, you might miss the opportunity for real dialogue and learn something important from the person you're speaking to.

Instead, think about your main points and your ultimate goals, practice listening, and stay flexible so you can adapt as needed during the conversation.

Empathy, sympathy, and compassion

I've talked a lot about being empathetic in communication because it truly helps get to an outcome that works for everyone the most quickly. There are a few nuances between empathy, sympathy, and compassion that are helpful to understand and harness at times.

Empathy is when you can deeply understand the feelings of another because you've had the same situation happen to you or you share a similar emotional system. Like people who suffer from anxiety can be empathetic to each other because they know what those all-night sessions seeking information from Dr. Google are about. Or those who have started a business know intimately about that labor of love that is entrepreneurship. It's, *"I know how you feel, I went (or go) through the same exact thing."*

Sympathy is when you can understand why a person would feel the way they do, and feel for them, but don't have first-hand experience. It's, *"I feel for you, and I can only imagine what this must be like for you."*

Compassion is often overlooked but a powerful mindset for connection without going down the rabbit hole of reliving your own emotions, which could be harmful to your balance. You care deeply, and will help, but are able to not let it keep you up at night.

When there is understanding, stress and conflict will automatically lower. This is your secret weapon when it comes to tough conversations.

Listen to understand

Too often, people go into difficult conversations ready to defend their point of view or get their message across, but real progress happens when we *listen to understand*, not just respond. More on this soon, but if you can set aside your own agenda and really hear what the other person is saying, you're more likely to find common ground and solutions.

Acknowledge and validate others' emotions

Even if you don't agree with everything the other person says, acknowledging and validating their emotions can go a long way. You can say something like, *"I understand that this situation is frustrating,"* or, *"It sounds like you're feeling overwhelmed, and I hear you."* Acknowledging and validating someone's perspective doesn't mean you're conceding the point, rather it shows that you recognize and respect their feelings, which can diffuse tension and make them more open to hearing your perspective.

Focus on solutions, not blame

Rather than focusing on who's at fault or what went wrong, direct the conversation toward how you can both move forward. When you approach the conversation with a mindset of collaboration, the other person is more likely to do the same.

Presume positive intent

Presuming positive intent means that when you're on the receiving end of a frustrating or negative action or behavior, like someone missing a deadline or sending a terse-sounding email, you stop yourself from assuming the worst. Instead of thinking, *"They're so lazy,"* or, *"They're being mean,"* redirect your thoughts and consider that their actions came from a place of good intention, or at minimum, were done with no ill intent.

This shift in perspective not only keeps you from spiraling into frustration, but creates space for curiosity, and it opens the door for a more productive conversation. This doesn't mean excusing someone's bad behavior if it's a pattern, but it does allow for a more balanced and empathetic approach, which is essential in a collaborative work environment.

When you assume positive intent, it doesn't just protect your own peace of mind, it also changes how others perceive and respond to you. This strategy aids in your balance because people are more willing to help and support you when you give them the benefit of the doubt, which fosters a more collaborative, trusting, and supportive workplace (aka, a place you enjoy working in versus wanting to run from when in burnout mode).

Effective communication is a two-way street

Communication consists of *two* parts: expressing yourself *and* listening to others.

Communicating isn't only about getting *your* ideas and concepts heard and acted upon; it also requires that you listen, understand, and take action on what other people say. When done right (more on this below), you'll find that effective communication can often be less about talking and actually more about listening.

Listening is just as important as expressing and isn't just about hearing what someone is saying in order for you to know what you want to say next, it's about really trying to understand their perspective.

Sometimes, people think they're being productive by constantly offering ideas or talking through solutions. But real progress often comes from slowing down and fully understanding the situation first.

Think about your most successful conversations. They have likely been when you've tuned into what the other person was saying versus giving them a monologue. Remember a time when someone really listened to you. Didn't it feel great when they made eye contact, nodded, and didn't rush to respond? That simple act of being heard makes you feel lighter and more connected. Even if the person you're talking to says nothing but is showing they're listening, you feel seen, heard, and understood.

I once had a colleague ask how I was doing during a particularly stressful week. Instead of giving the standard "I'm fine," I admitted I was feeling extra pressure with a project I was working on. She didn't try to solve it—she just looked me in the eye and said, "You've got this. Let me know how I can support you." That small acknowledgement made all the difference. In the workplace, moments like this create trust and reduce stress, which all aid in more productive and collaborative interactions and relationships (aka, more balance for you!).

Listening creates space for curiosity. When you're not just waiting for your turn to speak, you're learning. This can completely change how you approach disagreements and conflicts. Even if you don't agree with the other person's point of view, asking questions to understand where they're coming from makes it easier to remain calm and open-minded.

Listen—when you're ready

You know how, in the office, we casually ask, *"How's it going?"* when we see a colleague walk by our desk. We often do this while we're in the middle of something else, without really being ready to listen to the answer.

Don't ask unless you're ready to listen.

Instead, try saying *"Hey, I'd love to hear how things are going and catch up. Let me finish this email and I'll be right with you."* That way, you're not just being polite and allowing yourself the time to make a mindset shift; you're setting the stage for a more quality connection.

It may feel like a person's call, text, or cubicle pop-by means you have to immediately respond, but you don't have to drop everything you're doing the second someone wants your attention or needs something from you. This includes your boss, team, parents, partner, friends, your kids, anyone.

This approach not only helps you stay balanced but also improves the quality of your conversations. When you're not distracted or resentful, your responses are more thoughtful, and the other person feels genuinely heard. Over time, people will become more mindful of when and how they approach you. Less interruption equals more peace and productivity. Yay for that!

Becoming the best listener

Now that you know why listening is a much-needed skill, let's go over how best to do it.

"Active listening" means that when someone is speaking to you, you are focused completely on them, absorbing and understanding their message, comprehending and integrating the information, and responding thoughtfully.

You're not just understanding the words or the information being communicated to you, but also the *intentions and underlying messages* behind what you hear.

Active listening doesn't always come naturally. It requires a conscious effort to understand what's being said, both in words and through nonverbal cues, so you can engage meaningfully together.

Here's how to do it.

1. **Face the person:** Turn your body toward the person talking to you and make eye contact to show you're fully engaged.
2. **Notice nonverbal signals:** Pay attention to body language and facial expressions as this is information they're telling you. *Are they tense? Open and loose? Are their arms crossed defensively? Are they rubbing their eyes as if they're tired or upset?*
3. **Don't jump into problem-solving mode:** Resist the urge to offer solutions unless you're asked. Sometimes people just need to be heard. Holding space by listening can be much more rewarding for the speaker than giving them advice. If they want advice, you can pretty much bet they'll

ask you for it. If you have a brilliant idea that you must share, ask if they want to hear it before just blurting it out. Say, *"I have an idea, would you like to hear it?"*

4. **Use nonverbal affirmations:** Simple gestures like nodding your head, smiling, and saying *"yes"* and *"uh-huh"* show you're listening and encourage the speaker to continue.

5. **Eliminate distractions.** If you can, silence your phone or even turn it off. If you're on a video call, don't try to check your email or play a game. You'll lose focus and the speaker will pick up on it. There are distractions you can ignore, and ones that need attention. If your phone dings with an urgent message from your kids' school nurse, openly say why. *"Excuse me, I need to check this; it's my kids' school. Can you give me a moment?"*

It's also helpful to set the stage before a conversation if you know you may be interrupted. For example, if you know a doctor will be calling with test results while you're on a call or in a meeting, tell the person the interruption might happen and why, so it's not jarring or disrespectful. This way, you can gracefully handle it by pausing the conversation and then transitioning back.

6. **Don't plan what you're going to say next while someone is talking.** If your attention is on what you're going to say, you aren't fully able to hear what is being said.

7. **Take notes, if needed.** In more elaborate discussions, if you want to take notes, tell or ask the person if they mind.

8. **Don't interrupt.** Allow the speaker to finish their thoughts to completion before you respond with your questions or thoughts.

9. **Repeat back.** Paraphrase what you've heard to make sure you understood them correctly. You can say, " What I'm hearing you say is _____. " Or, "I want to make sure I understand _____, can you repeat _____?"

This not only clarifies the message but also validates the speaker's feelings or thoughts.

10. **Ask questions.** To show you're engaged, ask clarifying questions like, *"What do you mean by that?"* or *"Can you tell me more about that?"* This deepens your understanding and encourages further dialogue.

11. **Seek first to understand instead of to be understood.** By being curious and showing interest in the other person's perspective, you gain their trust and they will share more honestly. Even if the subject matter is boring or offensive to you, keep in mind that you can always be interested by being curious, supporting the other person, learning something new, and being open-minded.

12. **Avoid judgment.** It's impossible to be empathetic if you're judging the person while they speak. Even subtle cues like eye-rolling or dismissive gestures can shut down a conversation. Keep an open mind, and approach disagreements with curiosity rather than judgment: *"That's interesting—what led you to that conclusion?"*

Extend respect, compassion, grace, and forgiveness to the degree that you would like it extended to you.

Understanding body language

We've all been in meetings or 1-on-1s where someone says all the right things, but something feels off. That's because non-verbal cues (body language, facial expressions, and eye contact) play a huge role in communication. **In fact, much of what we "hear" in a conversation doesn't come from the words themselves but from *how* they're delivered.**

Read the room. In meetings, pay attention to how people are sitting. Are they leaning forward, engaged, or are they slouched back, arms crossed, signaling disinterest or resistance? In 1-on-1s, watch for things like eye contact. Are they maintaining it, showing they're present, or avoiding it, possibly signaling discomfort or distraction? These non-verbal cues provide insight into the real dynamics at play.

One of the quickest ways to create confusion is when your words and body language don't align. Imagine telling someone, *"I'm really excited about this project,"* but your arms are crossed, and you're avoiding eye contact. The mixed signals will make it hard for them to trust what you're saying. This is where the concept of *congruence* comes in, ensuring that your non-verbal cues match your words.

A fun way to illustrate this is to practice saying something negative while smiling. For example, say, *"I really hate this idea,"* with a big grin on your face. It doesn't feel right or look right, does it? The tone and expression are more impactful than the words themselves, leaving the listener confused.

One significant study, Mehrabian's Rule[26], backs this up. It found that when verbal and non-verbal communication doesn't match, people tend to trust the non-verbal signals more. So, if your words say one thing but your body language says another, people are more likely to believe the latter. If you want to be clear and credible, make sure your non-verbal communication is backing up your message.

Feedback as a tool for connection and success

How to *give* feedback

Giving feedback shouldn't be reserved for annual or semiannual reviews. **Effective feedback happens regularly and in real-time.**

Think of feedback like coaching a sports team: a baseball coach wouldn't wait until the end of the season to correct a player's swing. They'd give feedback in the moment so the player can adjust, improve, and perform better the next time they go up to bat. The same goes for managers and colleagues in a professional setting.

When it comes to giving feedback, the goal should always be to help the other person grow, not just point out what's wrong. To do this effectively, your feedback needs to be specific, actionable, and focused on *behaviors*, not personalities.

So instead of saying, *"You're not pulling your weight on the team,"* try something like, *"I've noticed the last two reports were submitted late, and it's causing delays. Let's discuss how we can improve the workflow to hit deadlines. Are there roadblocks or other issues in the way that I can help with?"*

This keeps the conversation focused on outcomes and improvements, rather than feeling like an attack.

Always tie feedback back to growth—*"This adjustment will help us all meet our targets and keep the project moving smoothly."* By framing it as an opportunity for development, you show that the intention is positive and forward-looking. And don't forget to follow up. Check in on progress and continue the dialogue, showing that feedback isn't a one-time thing but part of an ongoing process.

How to *receive* feedback

Receiving negative feedback, even if it's intended to be helpful, can be tough, especially if it touches on areas that are sensitive for us. Imagine you've been working extra long hours on a project, giving it your proverbial (and maybe even literal) blood, sweat, and tears, and after submitting it to your manager, their first response is "You have a bunch of typos." In the grand scheme of things, typos aren't a big deal, but you just put your heart into this, and that one piece of feedback can feel like a gut punch.

Try to listen openly, without getting defensive. Pause and absorb what they're saying (yes, this is hard.). Resist the urge to immediately explain yourself or push back. **Your first job is to understand their perspective.** A simple response like, *"Thank you* *for sharing this, I'll make sure to check for typos before sending the next draft,"* or *"Thank you for your feedback, I'll take some time to think it over,"* shows maturity and willingness to learn.

If the feedback isn't clear, ask questions to better understand: *"Can you give me an example of where you've seen this happen?"* This turns the conversation into a learning moment rather than a confrontation. Remember, feedback is a tool for your growth, even if it stings at first. Use it to improve, not to fuel self-doubt or frustration.

When you disagree with the feedback. There will be times when you disagree with the feedback you hear, or feel that the feedback you get isn't warranted. Maybe you got called out for double-booking your boss, but you had scheduled your meeting before someone else scheduled a conflicting meeting that you weren't informed about. If your boss comes to you saying that you need to do better with your scheduling, you can kindly respond by sharing that you understand their frustration, that your meeting was scheduled first, and you'll double-check with them going forward.

This is a common occurrence for new hires in particular, as they're acclimating to a new work environment and learning what the cultural norms are (i.e., that everyone checks with the boss via a direct message before scheduling a meeting). If you get called out for something that you were ill-informed about, you can point out what might help you do your best job in the future, like in the example of a new hire, that cultural norms be included as part of the onboarding process to prevent this from being an issue for others.

This tactic works on a personal level as well. I have a tendency to add events to our personal calendar—dinners with friends, and weekend events—without checking with Kyle. He once got frustrated with me when I'd made brunch plans on a Saturday after he'd been traveling for a week doing client work. Instead of me reacting with *"This is the only day/weekend we'll have available for the next four months!*," I said, "*I totally understand. I imagine you'll be tired after having been on the road all week. This is the only day that we and the Nelsons have availability for the next four months. Would you like me to cancel it? I'll make sure to check with you before adding social plans to our calendar going forward.*"

Navigating email and messaging overload

Oh, the bittersweet nature of digital devices and real-time communication. It can be so fulfilling to take care of business from your phone, and yet so stressful. When your inbox is overflowing, direct message notifications keep pinging, and you're juggling multiple threads of communication all day, it's no wonder you can feel so scatterbrained at the end of the day.

Managing digital overload starts with prioritization and setting up a dedicated time to respond to messages. Not every email needs an immediate response. Set clear expectations with your team about response times.

For example, establish that urgent requests should be flagged with a subject line or a direct message, (like discussed above) while non-urgent ones can wait. Block off time in your calendar to check emails and messages, rather than constantly reacting to notifications. (Efficiency win!) This way, you stay focused on your tasks instead of being pulled in every direction by the latest ping.

Also, don't hesitate to use tools like folders, filters, and automated replies to keep things organized. Your goal is to avoid getting sucked into the endless cycle of digital noise while still staying responsive where it matters.

I do this personally in a variety of ways:

1. **My email signature includes language** that I work in time blocks and check my email twice per day.
2. **When I'm traveling or working on a project that requires deep focus, I enable an automatic/vacation responder**

message stating what I'm up to and that I will respond as soon as I can.

3. **I "snooze" certain emails for days and times when I will be ready to read and/or respond to them.** For example, I schedule non-urgent emails that need reviewing, to return to my inbox on Friday mornings.

4. **I have folders named "Action Required" and "Awaiting Response"** where I place appropriate emails so I can easily find what I need when I need it.

Virtual meetings and presentations

In virtual meetings, engagement can easily slip, which can lead to unnecessary stress later when either you or your team has missed important information.

Keeping people engaged in a video conference requires a little extra effort. Start by doing a 3-minute standup comedy routine (I'm kidding, sort of!)

Start by setting a clear agenda and, as we addressed above, keeping the meeting concise. No one wants to sit through a two-hour video call unless Jack Black is hosting it. Just like in-person meetings, kick it off with a personal check-in, or do a climate-setting exercise. One of my favorites is "this or that" where you ask someone a "this or that" question, and they answer and turn to another person and do a new "this or that." For example, *"Beach or Mountains?" "Coffee or Tea?" Dogs or Cats?"* As simple as it sounds, this activity makes meetings more personable and offers a moment of levity with humor as well. During the meeting, encourage participation by asking questions, calling on participants by name, and using interactive tools like polls or shared documents.

You may be wondering what weighing in on if you prefer cats or dogs before a budget meeting has to do with reducing burnout. Intentionality and awareness around how and when we connect with each other all contribute to our feelings of balance and calm, and/or our feelings of burnout, stress, and overwhelm. Moments of connection, even with a little "this or that" can bring a smile to your meeting that maybe you wouldn't have had otherwise, adding a little sparkle to a potentially otherwise very rote and stressful day.

Roles and responsibilities communication

It can be so stressful to work hard on a task only to find out someone else had done it or it wasn't what was needed from you. **Understanding roles and responsibilities avoids confusion and ensures the smoothest outcomes possible— whether at work or at home.** When everyone knows exactly what's expected of them, things run like a well-oiled machine, with fewer surprises and less stress.

At work, this means getting clarity from the start about who's responsible for what, whether it's on a project, in a meeting, or in day-to-day tasks. It's never too late to get that clarity. No matter what position you have or where you are in a project, you can initiate a conversation and connect with your team about roles and responsibilities.

Additionally, it can be helpful not just to state what every individual will do, but also what they *won't* do. Knowing what *isn't* your responsibility is just as important as knowing what *is*. Too often, we take on tasks or problems that aren't really ours to handle. When roles and responsibilities are clearly defined, they help you stay in your lane, focusing on what you need to do without feeling the pressure to fix everything.

Let's say you're leading a project at work, but instead of focusing on your role—managing the timeline and ensuring deliverables—you start stepping into your team's responsibilities, like tweaking designs or handling scheduling tasks. Not only does this distract you from your core duties, but it also disempowers your team. By sticking to your role and trusting your team to handle theirs, the project runs smoother, and you avoid unnecessary pressures and stress, and duplicative efforts.

This applies at home too. If you've ever dealt with the chaos of household duties getting mixed up or neglected, you know how important it is to clarify who's in charge of what. Just like at work, setting clear roles at home—whether it's managing the kids' schedules or splitting household chores—helps avoid unnecessary stress and conflict with your family members.

Here is a checklist to get everyone in the right state of mind before a responsibilities discussion:

1. **Remember, you are first and foremost a team**: You're here to support each other and work together towards the same team and company goals.
2. **Bring a list of everything you handle:** Writing out all your tasks will remind you of how much you contribute and I guarantee you'll feel like a superhero when you see this list. Your calendar items can help inform this list.
3. **Share and evaluate your lists:** At the meeting, share your lists with the team and evaluate them together. Estimate how much time each task takes and discuss if the workload feels balanced, equitable, and appropriate based on skill levels, expertise, and role. This will help everyone understand the bigger picture and make adjustments as needed.
4. **Factor in the emotional importance of certain tasks:** Some tasks may hold more emotional value for certain team members. For example, if someone has a personal connection to a specific client or project, they might be more motivated to handle that responsibility.
5. **Consider strengths and weaknesses:** Consider each team member's strengths and weaknesses. Maybe someone hates dealing with scheduling, while someone

else loves crossing off tasks like that—it's a win-win when you can trade off responsibilities that align with individual preferences.

6. **Discuss when and how tasks should be done**: Go beyond just assigning roles—talk about timelines and methods too. For example, if the team knows a report is always finalized by Friday, it avoids last-minute chaos.

And finally, the most important step:

7. **What isn't on your list—let it go:** Seriously, let it go. Trust your team members to handle their responsibilities, and don't waste energy worrying about what's not on your plate. If someone struggles, they should feel comfortable reaching out for help. You're not responsible for everything.

If things don't get done to your liking, remind yourself that not everything needs to be done *your way*. If a certain task is really meaningful to you, it's worth revisiting the responsibilities conversation to see if a trade makes sense. Otherwise, it's time to let go and trust the process.

Cultural nuances

In addition to each person's unique conversation and communication style based on their background, experiences, and perspective, different cultures communicate in different ways, too. Diversity within an organization is one of the most valuable assets it can have, and bringing people together of varying cultures can sometimes create unintentional conflict. What means one thing in one country could mean a very different thing in another.

I experienced this firsthand when I interviewed a potential hire from Brazil. At the end of the interview, I gave the "okay" hand symbol 🤏 after saying that I would get back to them soon with the next steps.

The interviewee didn't have the same association with that gesture and offensively responded, "Excuse me!" Apparently in Brazil, that gesture is the equivalent of extending the middle finger. Oops!

In some cultures, being direct and upfront is often valued, while in others, preferred communication can be more subtle and indirect, with a focus on maintaining harmony. **When working with folks in areas of the world where you may not know the cultural ins and outs, keep an open mind, presume positive intent, and politely ask for clarification when needed.** Like: *"To make sure I'm understanding correctly, you are asking for XYZ."*

Communication obstacle: Ego

If you want more productive communication, never let your ego lead the way. Ego can turn small disagreements into full-out battles. Even if you *know* you're right, most of the time it's better to be supportive and listen than to emphasize your being right. This is easier said than done.

Imagine a colleague calling you out for not sharing critical information on a project. Your first reaction might be, *"They've done the same thing to me dozens of times!"* That's ego talking. But instead of reacting, take a breath and recognize this is their moment to express their frustration, and it's not yours to retort on their past behaviors. Acknowledge their feelings, listen, and remember it's not about proving your point. It's about finding a resolution.

In that moment, instead of snapping back, you could say, *"You're right. I didn't share the information, and I can see how that's frustrating for you."* Owning your part can turn what could have been a long, drawn-out argument into a quick, constructive conversation. You've avoided hours of stress and frustration by putting your ego aside and choosing to focus on a solution rather than escalating the conflict. And, there's an opportunity to share back to them if and when they omit information next time.

When you handle confrontation without letting your ego take over, you create space for resolution. We've all seen how quickly workplace conflicts can escalate when people are wrapped up in defending their egos. But when you leave the ego out, you allow for honest communication, quicker resolutions, and a more peaceful work environment.

This doesn't mean there won't be disagreements or tense moments, but it does prevent many unnecessary big, blow-out confrontations that waste time and energy. By owning up to mistakes and offering genuine apologies, you build trust and goodwill. And when you model that behavior, others will follow. Your colleagues will appreciate your willingness to take responsibility, and they'll feel more comfortable doing the same.

The ego is tied to our sense of self and often grabs a megaphone at the worst possible times. But by practicing understanding, compassion, respect, and trust in positive intent, you can keep your ego from taking the wheel and steering the conversation.

When recognizing and combating the ego's ugly head, you make space for respect in your relationships. At the core of healthy communication is respect, and it works both ways. Even if you disagree, allowing colleagues or team members to speak their truth without interrupting or invalidating their feelings, signals that you respect them. In the same way you want to be heard, give others space to share. Avoid defensive responses like, *"That's not true!"* or *"How could you think that?"* as well as extreme words like "never" and "always." These reactions immediately shut down meaningful and constructive conversations. Instead, try saying something like, *"I hear you, and I respect where you're coming from. Let's work on making sure we're both on the same page moving forward."* Respect goes a long way when prioritizing your peace and calm at work.

Communication wrap-up

Whether you're in a leadership position or not, you can lead by example when it comes to effective communication. And if you *are* in a leadership role, your behavior speaks louder than words and will inspire more cultural change than any company policy.

✓ **Explain the "why" to reduce misunderstandings**. Explaining the "why" behind requests helps others understand and support your decisions.

✓ **Be clear**. Clear, concise messaging prevents information overload and reduces decision fatigue.

✓ **Start listening more**. Active listening is just as important as speaking; it involves understanding the speaker's intentions, not just their words.

✓ **Respond, don't react**. Take a moment before responding to ensure a thoughtful, respectful, and productive conversation.

✓ **Assertive communication is the sweet spot**. Balancing your needs with respect for others allows for clearer boundaries and healthier workplace dynamics.

✓ **Leave your ego at the door.** This allows for more productive, helpful resolutions.

✓ **Set boundaries on digital communication.** This way, you're not running around reacting to messages all day.

✓ **Give and receive feedback, kindly.** Be clear and allow for a two-way dialogue.

✓ **Managing conflict.** When expecting conflict, prepare for what could happen. And when in conflict, before any damage is done, you can take a break and come back to it another time.

Communicating well with colleagues and leaders in your organization, as well as those closest to you increases balance and nurtures healthier relationships by lessening misunderstandings, creating visibility, and assigning ownership on who does what, ensuring everyone is on the same page. Next, we'll explore how being mindful and intentional about the people you spend time with and whom you communicate with regularly can make or break your balance.

Community

Strong connections, a supportive culture, and collaboration methods to improve well-being

"If you want to go fast, go alone. If you want to go far, go together."

— *African Proverb*

It's six in the evening. Your phone lights up—your boss just messaged that tomorrow's 9 a.m. presentation has been moved up to 8 a.m., and they need last-minute revisions on the deck.

You sigh, staring at the pile of unread emails in your inbox. You were about to shut down for the day. But now? Dinner will have to wait (which will upset your partner). And the same with the gym, when you'd promised yourself you'd exercise after work. *Oh well*, you think. You dive back into work mode, trying to juggle the revisions while fielding texts from a team member who finally started replying to critical questions after being radio silent all day. Additionally, yet another message comes in from a colleague in a different time zone, asking if you can "quickly" jump on a call to troubleshoot a completely unrelated issue. *I don't have time for this!* you think. You can feel your pulse rising. Your mind is racing. Thoughts pummel your nervous system: *How did I get stuck with all of this? Why am I always the one holding things together? This is too much.*

You try to shake it off and focus, but you're interrupted again— this time by a client who just flagged an issue with the numbers on the report you sent earlier this week. You feel the pressure mounting. It's overwhelming. Your chest tightens. *What if I miss a deadline? What if I mess this up?* You fire off a message to your work buddy, saying, simply: "This report is so messed up, I'm never going home tonight!"

A few minutes pass, and your phone buzzes again, this time from your buddy. "Send me the report, I'll review it; I'm working late too." This was just the boost you needed. With that message, you feel the weight lift slightly. Your colleague gets it and has your back, and now you feel like you can manage one thing at a time.

This is the power of community at work.

In this chapter, we'll explore why building a strong support network is essential for maintaining balance, assessing your current community, ensuring you have the right people around you, and nurturing it to support your balance. I'll review how to find, filter, and choose allies who will support you, and how to distance yourself from those who drain your energy. Because in your career, just like in life, the right community can help you not only survive but also thrive.

Community for balance

Having a few trusted people who you can be real with and who care to share your challenges when things get tough lightens your emotional load. By sharing what's going on for you, you release the burden of carrying all of your emotions and stressors around with you at all times. These trusted people are a place where you can set these things down, even if only momentarily. I'm lucky to have Kyle as my rock, with whom I can share everything and feel seen, and I've also worked hard to build friendships and professional relationships where I can seek advice, connection, or just unwind.

Humans are wired for connection.[27] We thrive when we support one another, and we need different perspectives and strengths to make our lives and society function well.

Corporate and entrepreneurial life can feel isolating, especially when you're juggling tight deadlines and there isn't a lot of time to bond between endless meetings, learning ever-changing team dynamics, or acclimating to new projects.

Modern hybrid and work-from-home models also make it increasingly difficult to have natural connection moments with colleagues. Gone are the lunch break coffee runs or cubicle eavesdropping and sharing. The result of this has led to more burnout than ever. Even if you love what you do, you're going to feel more drained at the end of the day without having any live, spontaneous, fun connection, or closeness at work.

Having a few people to confide in at work, whether for advice, perspective, or just venting, goes a long way to help you leave work stress exactly where it belongs, at work, and not take it home to your pets, roommates, partner, and kids.

Community in the workplace

Building community at work goes beyond just having a team bonding exercise now and again. It's about being able to trust, confide, and count on each other. The best kind of work community is one where you can openly collaborate, brainstorm, give and receive honest feedback, and have a trusting, safe space to vent when things get overwhelming.

Imagine a workplace where colleagues uplift each other, recognize each other's talents and wins, and laugh at the inside jokes only possible within your particular organization. Once I witnessed a push-up contest on the 7th floor of a skyrise, and while it seemed like we were "goofing off," we all worked better and harder after sharing those laughs.

The most successful projects and teams I've been on and led have had more than just the right skill sets on the team—

they had the right people. And oftentimes, teammates you respect and collaborate with turn into friends as well. Relationships like those often outlast the job itself, and I can say some of my closest friends today are people I met at work.

In my first job out of college, I worked at a preschool as the Director's assistant. There was a new assistant teacher, Rachel, and we quickly bonded. We took lunch breaks together, bounced ideas off each other, vented about the administration, and shared frustrations over the typical challenges of the job—she kept me sane when my boss did things that drove me up the wall. Our friendship moved outside of work, and eventually, she became such an important part of my life that she was a bridesmaid at my wedding eight years after we first met.

Belonging and collaboration

We all want to feel like we belong, and that need doesn't disappear just because we're at work. In fact, and research supports this—people are more likely to quit their jobs due to poor relationships with colleagues than hating the job itself.[28] Think about the favorite jobs you've had, was it the work or the people that made it memorable and enjoyable? And when you think about your least favorite jobs, did you hate your tasks and responsibilities or was there conflict and tension with your coworkers? Or worst of all, a mix of both!

When you dislike or feel disconnected from the people you spend the majority of your day with, getting through the day can feel agonizing, like the character Luis Litt on the show Suits. Throughout the show, we witness Luis struggling with feeling excluded, undervalued, resentful, and disconnected from his colleagues. Spoiler alert: He so badly wants to be accepted and have camaraderie at work that he almost resigns in season two because he feels so unseen and underappreciated.

On the other hand, when you feel a sense of belonging, connected to, and respect with your teams, you're more likely to have a positive attitude, better performance, and be motivated and energized, like the effervescent Leslie Knope in the show, Parks and Recreation, whose camaraderie with colleagues like Ron and Ben make a workday fly by. Isn't it more fun and fulfilling to accomplish goals with your friends who have your back versus trying to reach a goal against others?

I've seen it firsthand, and I'm sure you have, too. In environments where collaboration is easy and supported at a cultural level, innovation and creativity thrive, and bonding between teammates comes naturally. In a team that works well together, the workload feels more manageable, and the stress of deadlines diminishes because you trust the people around you. Everyone is rowing in the same direction, and you're not navigating alone.

Your professional community

I remember working on a particularly high-stakes project, an out-of-state event for investors for a property my asset management company had acquired—we had tight deadlines and tons of moving parts. One of my colleagues and I were in charge of all the event logistics including timeline, transportation, and lodging for the investors. We had to research and employ numerous vendors, and it did *not* all go smoothly. Endless and last-minute calls and emails making changes left and right from investors, vendors, logistical partners, and more in the days and weeks leading up to the event made for a chaotic set of moving pieces. What got us through wasn't just our individual expertise; it was the way we rallied around each other, covering gaps and pushing through challenges as a team. That camaraderie made all the difference in our success.

As you can imagine, resilience and adaptability increase when you're part of a supportive team. Studies show that employees who feel supported are more likely to persevere during high-stress periods, as their team acts as a buffer against burnout and enables faster recovery and adjustment to new circumstances.[29]

Your personal community

As mentioned earlier, we all have one life, and while it's common to categorize "work" separately from "home" life, they affect each other. For example, if you've argued with your partner in the morning, that energy follows you into your work day. And if you've shared a hearty laugh with your partner over breakfast, you bring that positive energy into the office. Suddenly, that report doesn't feel so daunting.

Personal connections and experiences outside of work fill your cup. They're reminders that you're not defined solely by your job or your performance at work. When you feel seen and supported in your personal life, the pressures of work don't weigh as heavy. Whether it's family, friends, or even a regular workout group or book club, these networks contribute to your emotional and mental health, making you more resilient to workplace stress.

I'll show you how to build and nurture the right communities for you, both personally and professionally, below.

How to be intentional about your community and friendships

Let's take a moment to assess your current community and feeling of belonging. Do you feel supported by your current network? Do you have a circle that genuinely looks out for you, both personally and professionally?

If you do, fantastic! And if not, don't worry, you're not stuck. To a large degree, you can choose your community. And, if you're like me, and you find yourself needing to start from scratch at any point in your life, you can.

When being intentional about the people you surround yourself with, whether you're just starting or assessing your current circles, it's important to have friends and colleagues who are not only supportive of your goals but also contribute positively to your overall well-being. If someone close to you isn't supportive or aligned with your (healthy and positive) goals or is a constant drain on your energy, it's time to make some decisions about who you spend your limited time and energy with.

To help you think about this, reflect on the following questions:

- What qualities do you desire in the people supporting you?
- Who are the people who help you to feel calm, bring you a sense of peace, and help you feel the most balanced, and why?
- Who depletes your energy and adds chaos to your life, and why?

We become much like the people we spend the most time with. Consider the qualities in people close to you—who do you want to be more like? Identify what the qualities are that you admire, and spend more time with those people.

When you're serious about building and prioritizing balance, part of the process is cutting down on, as much as possible, elements, including people, that aren't healthy for you. This isn't always possible with family or coworkers, but if they consistently bring you stress and disruption, it's important to limit time spent with them and/or the power of their influence.

This may sound harsh, but being selective about who you spend your time with isn't selfish, it's necessary for your well-being. Letting go of a friendship, especially one with a long history, is tough. It's a lot easier to talk about it than actually do it. I've been there, both personally and professionally. It's never easy to distance yourself from someone you were once close to.

Even if you're pulled toward people pleasing, remember that other people's happiness is not your responsibility. You are not your friends' and colleagues' therapist or caretaker, and it's okay to (kindly) step away from or distance yourself from a relationship that is depleting you. Even if you can't completely sever ties, you can change how you engage with those people to limit their impact on you.

On my journey, I've had to learn to be intentional about who I allow into my life and who I spend my limited time and energy with, especially after moving to San Francisco, with four kids, a business, and a traveling husband.

As someone naturally inclined to help and nurture, it wasn't immediately easy to see who added value and who drained me. But by assessing each relationship through the lens of balance and well-being, I've learned to make those difficult decisions about where to invest my time and energy.

I had to do this in all areas of life when building a new community for myself and my family, in addition to the people Kyle and I would bring into our company to support our vision and purpose of Be Courageous. It was all a learning curve, that was not without trials and errors.

I acknowledge that not everyone reading this book has the luxury to make decisions about who they work with, but there tends to be a lot more freedom with who you choose to spend time outside of work.

With the mindset of balance as a driving force in your community decision-making, it's much easier to distinguish who adds to your feelings of equilibrium and those who throw you off balance.

Steps to create distance in unhealthy relationships

If you find that a relationship isn't serving you, whether temporarily or indefinitely, you don't have to cut ties completely. You can create distance in ways that feel manageable. For example:

- **Limit one-on-one time**: Shift to group hangouts rather than one-on-one meetups.
- **Set boundaries**: Let them know you're going through a busy time and won't be able to connect as often. You don't need to explain further.
- **Control communication**: Don't feel obligated to respond immediately when they reach out. Keep responses neutral and avoid asking follow-up questions that keep the conversation going.
- **Shift the dynamic**: Over time, the person will likely seek out someone else to fill the space you used to occupy.

Creating space in these relationships doesn't have to be abrupt or dramatic. You can let the person know that you need space right now and that you'll reach out when you're ready to connect again. Or, gradually reduce the frequency and depth of your interactions. Most people will naturally sense the shift and adjust accordingly.

Finally, here's a powerful question to ask yourself when evaluating a relationship: *If I met this person today, would I choose to spend time with them?* If the answer is no, it's time to reassess the role they play in your life. As you work hard to create peace, joy, and balance in your world, make sure you're sharing that space with the right people—the ones who support your peace, energize you, and align with your values.

Navigating a toxic workplace "community"

I put the word "community" in quotes because my definition of community implies a healthy atmosphere. But if you find yourself in a toxic work environment, assess the bigger picture of your workplace. *Are there other people who you can connect with? New people you can meet? Can you limit interactions with toxic people?* Maybe you need to move desks or go to lunch at a different time so you won't see these people in the break room. If the entire environment is toxic, maybe it would make sense to move to a different team, department, or company altogether. That is a much bigger topic for a different time; the point is, you have choices.

How to create community at work

Mentorship

Two ways to use mentorship to enhance your community at work are to:

1. Ask for it.
2. Give it.

When it comes to mentorship, I've found that not many people ask for it. Oftentimes, ego is big in the workplace and many don't want to be seen as naive or needing help or have the idea that one must figure everything out on their own to grow and learn. But asking for mentorship is not a sign of weakness or naivety, it's a sign of strength, self-awareness, a desire for growth, and maturity in knowing that others are more knowledgeable and experienced and have much to offer.

Giving mentorship is another way to grow your community. If you encounter a colleague who is good at what they do, has room for growth, and shows strong potential, make an offer to mentor them. It shows them you're invested in their success. Plus, you'll gain insights into areas you wouldn't have access to otherwise. Finally, mentoring allows you to build (a new, different) rapport with someone you wouldn't have otherwise connected with. Put yourself in their shoes. How amazing would it have been if a leader noticed you and your potential and offered to mentor you?

By being a mentor and mentee, you'll also be more likely to be considered for promotions, and get support in your workplace trajectory, as people will see that you're seeking growth and willingly help others on their journeys as well.

The best leaders have mentors and are also mentors themselves.

Communicate your needs and allow for help

When needs arise, which they inevitably do because you can't do everything yourself, ask your community for support (that is the beauty of having one!). Asking for help is not a sign of weakness or lack of capability, it shows that you value collaboration. It also shows that you value others' opinions, skills, and superpowers, and prioritize teamwork.

Simultaneously, when someone offers help, assess your situation and accept the help when appropriate. If you don't need support, of course, gracefully decline, but be gracious for the offer. Say that you appreciate the offer and that you'll reach out if you want or need their skillset and perspective in the future. A genuine response is the best response.

People want to help. Accepting help allows you to participate in the virtuous circle of asking for and giving help.

Share about your personal life to connect with others

By sharing what you have going on outside of work, you build trust, rapport, and closeness with others. When your colleagues see you as more than just your role in the business, it humanizes you and makes you more likable. Think of a leader who talks about their kids, hobbies, personal goals, or trips they've taken. You end up feeling like you know them better and relate to them. You discover that you have more in common and that builds empathy, compassion, and understanding. For example, if you and your coworker both have kids ages two and six, you can relate to each other about elementary school transitions, early reading struggles, or potty training. If you both love surfing, you can talk about the swells you caught last weekend.

One time I shared with a colleague I didn't know well that Kyle was out of town for nine days. She offered to edit a presentation for me knowing that my evenings were stacked with kid responsibilities, and I gladly accepted!

Join or start an Employee Resource Group (ERG)

Attract and grow your work community by gathering with colleagues in scenarios that have nothing to do with your role. Employee resource groups (ERGs) are a great way to meet and build relationships with people who share commonalities outside of your role and responsibilities. These groups are typically formed to support diversity, inclusion, and belonging within the workplace, often representing specific communities or interests. Here are some examples of common ERGs: Groups for Parents and Caregivers, LGBTQ+, Disability/Accessibility, Veterans/Military, Multicultural/Diversity, Young Professionals/NextGen, Mental Health & Well-being, Sustainability/Green, Faith-Based, Allies, Generational, and racial and ethnicity-based groups like Black/African American, Hispanic/Latinx, and Asian/Pacific Islander.

This is also an opportunity to think back to the purpose work we talked about in the efficiency chapter. There could be alignment between an ERG group you join or start and your personal purpose.

Volunteering

You can also join (or create) a group for volunteering. Some companies offer community engagement days throughout the year where the workforce all volunteer at a particular collection of nonprofit organizations and local charities to support the local community.

You don't have to know every group member personally to feel you belong. Say hello. Ask for other people's names and introduce yourself. You slowly (or sometimes quickly) get to know each other and increase the number of friendly faces you see around the office (or on Zoom/Teams and in chats).

Say yes to social events (when you can)

In any professional setting, there are other gatherings like social hours, networking events, and coffee and chats where you can meet new people, spend time with people you don't interact with regularly, and build relationships.

Start a group or social event

Invite a colleague you don't know well out for a coffee break together. While doing HR at Juicy Couture, I took a risk and invited a colleague from PR to have lunch with me, and then invited her and her boyfriend over for dinner to my and my boyfriend's apartment. It was wonderful and made for a beautiful friendship and extra camaraderie in that we could talk about work and more when spending time together.

Special note for small companies

If you work within or run a small business, perhaps a family-owned operation, or a business with just a few employees, you can still build camaraderie and connection. Here are some ideas:

1. Set up your own company "holidays" that are meaningful to you and your team. Perhaps it is a Friday lunch where you bring lunch in (or virtually, allow everyone to expense a food delivery), and meet to chat and celebrate the week.
2. Gather your small team to join a larger network event that aligns with your industry.
3. Encourage everyone to sign up to further a work-related skill and meet after to share what they learned.

Setting the community example

If you're a leader in your organization, you are in a particularly great position to facilitate more connections within not only your team but across your company. You can create an environment where connection and collaboration thrive. Initiate team-building activities, and encourage cross-departmental interactions, mentorship, and peer support programs.

You can also partner with HR, People Operations, or your People Experience partner to facilitate more structured programs, like internal networking events, professional development workshops, or "lunch and learn" sessions that bring different teams together. These programs can break down silos, foster collaboration, and help team members form connections that go beyond their typical interactions.

Additionally, empower your team to take ownership of building community by asking them who would be interested in leading social events or team-building exercises. This not only creates more opportunities for bonding but also gives your team a sense of agency in shaping the work culture. Leaders can lead by example by attending these events, promoting inclusivity, and encouraging informal meetups to strengthen the workplace community.

I used to work for a global company where everyone worked remotely. One of the employees asked if I could create or facilitate an experience or exercise to help everyone get to know each other better. It was a fun opportunity, considering there were employees in Singapore, India, Canada, the UK, the Netherlands, all over the US, and more. Knowing the person who asked was a fierce competitor, I created a "get to know your colleagues" game where I sent everyone a list of questions like, *"What was your first job?"*, *"Where were you born?"*, and, *"What's a skill you have that no one at work knows about?"* From the answers, I created trivia questionnaires and sent them out quarterly to the entire organization. People spent hours researching their colleagues to figure out who had nine siblings, who had released a solo artist singer-songwriter album, and who had a trophy for their skills in ping-pong. It was a blast and bonding for the entire team to learn fun facts about the people they work with.

At the same company, the head of Communications would send out a message every time her team completed a project, shouting out each member's contribution. It was a fantastic way of highlighting individuals and celebrating their wins with everyone.

Professional community resources

You likely picked up this book because you're seeking tools to manage stress and avoid burnout. **Many strategies here will help you feel more grounded and balanced, but when chronic stress takes hold, it's often necessary to get support from someone who isn't connected to your work, family, or personal life.** This objective voice—whether it's a therapist, coach, or counselor—can help you see your situation from a new angle. They can offer insight that even your closest friends, family, or colleagues might miss because they have an objective perspective and aren't involved in your life.

Speaking to someone "without skin in the game" gives you the freedom to express what's really on your mind without fear of being misunderstood. You don't have to worry that they'll misconstrue your words or intentions, or attach their own biases and emotions to your words. You can explore thoughts, test them out, and realize that some are true, some are not true, and some are symptoms of deeper issues. This process is incredibly freeing, allowing you to release emotional baggage and uncover the underlying causes of your stress.

I sought a therapist a few years back when I was having a particularly tough season. Work stress was at an all-time high, and it was a particularly challenging time within my family. I talked to trusted friends about what was going on, and while they were incredibly supportive and validating, I wanted to talk to someone who didn't know me or my situation at all, who would be able to listen to me go over concerns and worries at length without getting fatigued at my venting the way a friend or family member might.

Additionally, I wanted to consult with someone who had the skills to see what I could not. Being that I'm a coach and self-development junkie, I already had a lot of self-help and mindset tools. I wanted to talk to someone who was an expert in the human mind and human experience. After a few sessions with a therapist, I expanded my knowledge and gained new ways to cope and grow within my family, helping everyone involved.

Community wrap-up

A strong, supportive, positive community fosters collaboration, empathy, and camaraderie, making professional and personal challenges more manageable. Through intentional relationship-building, you can cultivate a support system that brings a sense of resilience, belonging, well-being, and balance.

✓ **Importance of connection**. Having strong communities both in and out of the workplace reduces burnout, and improves resilience by providing a sense of belonging and emotional support. Special attention should be placed on fostering connection in remote and hybrid work cultures in particular, as these environments increase feelings of isolation.

✓ **Building workplace community**. Collaboration helps support a sense of belonging, increases morale, and enhances overall performance and well-being. Having colleagues you can talk to or rely on can also lighten your emotional load.

✓ **Intentional relationships**. Choose to have people in your network and foster connections that promote and support your well-being, calm, and balance, and distance yourself from those who drain your energy or distract you from your purpose.

✓ **Mentorship.** Mentoring someone or asking someone to mentor you is a win-win situation for community-building.

✓ **Leading by example**. Foster community by creating and promoting team-building activities, initiating mentorship, and providing opportunities for genuine togetherness.

✓ **External support benefits.** Consulting with a professional (like a coach or therapist) can offer an objective, expert, fresh perspective.

Now that you have the tools you need to build rapport, gain trust, and communicate your needs, you can use it all to create and protect space for your self-care, which is the next and final chapter.

Self-Care

The foundation for daily and long-lasting peace, productivity, and performance

"Self-care is giving the world the best of you, instead of what's left of you."

—Katie Reed

We've all heard about how important self-care is, but the real message is this: Self-care is absolutely *essential* if you want to show up as your best self at work (and everywhere else). The entirety of this book is in service of self-care—creating the space for it, protecting it— because without it, burnout is inevitable.

Self-care practices nurture you at your core and give you the foundation to show up as your most balanced, grounded self in every aspect of your life.

We all have practices, and rituals that restore us. Think about what you do that makes your spirit happy, that makes you feel connected to your deeper self, where you lose track of time, that evaporates stress and brings you peace. Self-care isn't about self-improvement, aspirations, or productivity, although they positively affect your personal growth and performance. It's about reconnecting with what makes you feel whole, and replenishing and sustaining your energy, so you can tackle whatever comes your way with clarity, calm, and focus.

You work harder when you feel better

A common myth about self-care is that it's not productive. This couldn't be further from the truth because when self-care is practiced regularly, you'll achieve even more than you do now. Productivity isn't about the number of hours you put in, it's how effectively you use that time. When well-rested and mentally clear, you'll get more quality work done in a shorter amount of time.

Making *you* a priority

Self-care isn't a new concept. Everywhere you turn, a product or service claims to be an essential part of your self-care routine: Bath bombs, candles, spa weekends. Heck, even car commercials use this as a sales tactic.

And sure, spas and new cars all sound great, but it's not practical or affordable for most, nor do they provide long-lasting effects towards your feelings of balance. You don't need to spend hundreds of dollars at the spa or go on a thousand-dollar fishing retreat to care for yourself. I'm talking about integrating mini self-care practices and rituals into your daily routines, which will be much more consistent and sustainable.

Self-care is finding and creating moments to recharge before, during, and after all the work you do for others.

Self-care practices shouldn't be implemented only once you're in the flames of burnout and have nothing left to give; use them to prevent the feeling altogether.

If you're anything like me, the idea of adding another "to-do" to your already packed day sounds exhausting. The last thing you need is another task. Don't worry, this isn't about creating more tasks.

In this chapter, I'll help you integrate self-care into your daily life in ways that don't feel like a burden or another to-do. With a little proactive energy, you can build small, sustainable self-care habits that will help you create more balance—both at work and at home.

Sustainable self-care is about finding small, daily things that give energy, add a smile, and lighten the burden. When you do that, everything else falls into place.

Here's a fun metric to consider, I created the self-care ratio– *Cost:Length of effect.* Consider the cost of the event/practice/ routine against the length of time it will provide you with feelings of calm and balance. This chapter provides you with food for fodder and practices that have a high ratio in favor of lasting calming effects. If the cost is high and the length of effect is low, I invite you to consider where your self-care investments could be better spent.

Self-care is up to you

As much as it'd be nice if our boss, partner, or friends could make us take care of ourselves (and certainly they can help), the only person who can really create the space for your self-care is the person in the mirror.

Only you can make yourself the priority. No one else can exercise, floss your teeth, or do a hobby for you. When you take care of yourself and make you a priority, you're better able to show up in your highest capacity for your team, family, and community. You can't do that and perform your best if you're burnt out or struggling. There are no medals for martyrs.

When I moved to the Bay Area with my husband and three kids (at the time), leaving my hometown and "village" of family and friends, I felt lost. New city, new job, no support system—it was like losing my identity overnight. I told Kyle I needed to figure things out. While he could support my efforts, it was up to me to create and protect the time to reconnect with and explore what energized me—physically, mentally, and spiritually.

During that process, I rediscovered what made me feel like me again, like meditation, hiking, and wearing big statement earrings. And found new self-care techniques for stress relief as well, like mini-dance parties and "bumblebee breath" (described later in this chapter). I found that when I made decisions from a place of choosing what helps me feel balanced everything more easily clicked—at home and work. I didn't leave everything else behind to care for myself. All I did was add myself to the list of priorities, not kick anything else off of it. As a result, I learned that prioritizing myself wasn't selfish and it made me a better partner, parent, and leader.

Proactive self-care

"Pay attention to the whispers, so you won't have to listen to the screams." This Cherokee proverb is about being proactive and preventing falling down from exhaustion.

Addressing issues when they're small before they escalate is a lot easier to remedy and saves you a lot of stress. We've all seen it - where small problems in a company, not attended to and left unchecked, snowball into bigger ones, especially as the business grows. When you address and rectify problems when they're small and more manageable, it prevents them from escalating, growing in complexity, and taking more time, effort, and resources to fix.

Think of the benefits of being proactive in terms of missing a deadline on a small project. If you brush it off as a one-time issue and ignore why it happened, it can easily become a pattern. Soon, your team could begin regularly missing deadlines, leaving clients frustrated. But if you address what happened early, ask questions, and offer support, you can fix the underlying issue—whether it's workflow, communication, or resources—before it turns into a bigger problem affecting your entire business.

The same goes for self-care. If you address burnout signs early—fatigue, frustration, or feeling overwhelmed—you prevent them from becoming something much bigger and harder to handle. Being proactive keeps work and other life issues and challenges manageable.

Self-care is a daily practice

Self-care is not a one-and-done, and balance is not a one-and-done.

Balance and its maintenance is a daily practice. The more you prioritize balance-inducing habits, the better you'll feel, and like exercise, the easier it will be to maintain momentum. Just like missing a workout doesn't erase all your hard work, skipping a day of self-care won't undo your efforts. The benefits of your routine stick with you, making it easier to bounce back after an off day.

The ripple effect of self-care

Setting a self-care example helps others do the same

Imagine the difference between having a boss who models setting and enforcing healthy boundaries and prioritizes physical exercise, versus a boss who burns the candle at both ends, modeling, quite literally, burnout. One might think, consciously or unconsciously "If my boss is doing it, it must be okay for me to do it, too" and most of the time, it is.

When you take care of yourself, you give other people permission to do the same. You don't have to say it explicitly; Just doing and being are enough to be influential. Imagine when you were a kid, if one of your parents got a babysitter once a week so they could go to a pottery class. That parent role modeled taking time to do something for themselves, which became a part of your view and belief system about parenting, and showed that weekly hobbies and self-interest nights are normal. It's the same at work. If you see your boss or colleague going for a walk or reading a novel during their lunch break, you see this as acceptable, and maybe even normal, and might feel inclined to do the same. Most likely another co-worker will see you walking or reading and will also start doing something self-sustaining during lunch break. The self-care ripple extends incredibly far, beyond what we could imagine.

Nurturing your body, mind, and spirit

When your body is well cared for, your mind is sharper, and your energy is higher. We've all had phases of life when we ate too much junk food or fast food out of convenience and took a break (intentional or not) from exercise. I know when that's happened to me, my momentum keeps me down and feeling like a lump. This could also apply to working excessive hours or spending too long "brain rotting" (as the teenagers these days call it) on social media. In that state, it's hard to do even basic thinking.

Physical and mental health are interconnected, and when you nurture one, the other tends to follow suit.

Listen to the signals

When your body or mind starts saying, "Hey man, you should take a rest," pay attention. You can't always control your schedule, but you can do a lot to prevent burnout by noticing and listening to your body and mind's signals.

And when you're in one of those magical moments where your energy is on fire—ideas are flowing, tasks are getting knocked out, or you're walking your fastest mile yet—ride that wave! Capitalize on your momentum!

A surprising energy-taker

Being social requires more energy than we often realize in many ways (physical, mental, and emotional). Interacting with people can be invigorating, whether it's networking with colleagues or engaging in an intellectual conversation. But it can also be draining.

After a big event—like hosting a workshop for executives or running a team meeting—my energy is often zapped. That's because we all have a "social energy bucket," and its capacity varies depending on the person and the situation.

If you're someone who needs alone time to recharge, schedule time in your calendar (remember the calendar?) before and after social events. Even if it means unwinding for 10 minutes in the car before and after meeting up with friends.

Magical sleep

We all know how important sleep is—whether from research or personal experience. Sleep is the ultimate recovery tool for both the mind and body, and it's the foundation for high performance and feeling balanced. Unfortunately, according to the CDC (Center for Disease Control), 35% of people don't get enough.[30]

When you're deprived of quality sleep, everything from your focus, to your mindset, to your ability to manage stress takes a hit. You may not even notice it at first. You might be so adaptable and good at masking the signs of exhaustion that no one (maybe not even you) can tell you're running on fumes. But—trust me, I've been here—there will be a moment when there aren't even fumes in your gas tank, and your body will shut down. There's an anonymous quote that says, *"If you don't make time for your wellness, you'll be forced to make time for your illness."* Getting shorter and snappy at your roommate? Are you feeling rage or intensely upset about minor things that wouldn't normally bother you, but are now super annoying? These can be symptoms of sleep deprivation.

When I was in my twenties, I felt invincible. I could hit the gym early, power through a full day of work, meet up with friends in the evening, stay out late, and repeat the next day. Oh boy, have things changed as I've gotten older. I no longer have the stamina of the Energizer Bunny and find myself needing to pace myself. If I have a big work event or presentation, I make sure to schedule lighter activities before and after. Whether it's a high-stakes meeting, workshop delivery, or a big networking event, I know I need downtime to recharge. Build in time for rest. Just like you would for any important meeting, block off time for sleep and downtime on your calendar.

What's your bedtime?

One way to get more sleep—and I hate to say it because I know you know this—is to simply hit the hay earlier. Easier said than done, I know. I love zoning out on a show or playing sudoku before bed. After all, this is finally your time! But that is precious sleep time you're wasting. Of course, you should unwind the way that soothes you but set a timer to limit the time and stick to it.

Another way to get your mind and body in a space to prepare for sleep is to create a nighttime routine to get the mind and body prepared for slumber. If you enjoy reading before bed, use a tangible book. Blue light emitted from devices disrupts the natural release of melatonin that helps the body naturally fall asleep. Studies show that limiting blue light exposure before bed helps with falling, staying asleep, and morning alertness.[31]

Red light on the other hand doesn't disrupt natural melatonin production and supports relaxation.[32] I was overjoyed when I learned this because Kyle usually goes to bed later than me and the lighting situation always made falling and staying asleep difficult. I would either leave the light on so that he could see when coming to our room, or he would turn it on or use his phone flashlight. Now that we have a red light bulb in a lamp in our bedroom, I leave that on for him when I go to bed, and he can sufficiently navigate pajamas, and avoid bonking into the dresser and bed frame.

Communicate your sleep need

One of the most effective ways I've found to try to get enough sleep (which is difficult with four kids and a husband who works in every time zone around the world) is by communicating my sleep needs with those around me. As discussed in the Communication chapter, be proactive.

If you're trying to establish a more consistent sleep routine, you can also let your team and colleagues know you'll be offline after a certain time. When I worked for a global non-profit, I'd get messages at all hours of the night. At first, I responded to messages whenever they came through, even if I saw a message at 3 a.m. When I intentionally decided to prioritize sleep, I told my colleagues that going forward I'd be offline between 7 p.m. and 7 a.m., and I adjusted my phone settings to silence notifications during those hours. At first, I felt guilty, but that guilt quickly turned to relief when I experienced the ease that came with having these boundaries and fewer dark sleep-deprived circles under my eyes.

Sleep as a parent and other extenuating factors

Once you become a parent, the days of going to bed when you want are long gone (don't worry, I'm told they come back someday, I hope) Before having a baby, sleeping was interrupted only by the sound of the alarm or natural body rhythms, and you didn't wake up startled by a four-year-old staring at you like a horror movie.

In addition to having kids, being a caregiver, or your own health needing extra time or care, there are other times in your career when you'll have to adjust your expectations around sleep. Maybe you're traveling for work or dealing with an intense project deadline that keeps you up late. Instead of fighting it, accept that your sleep might not be perfect during these periods and prioritize rest where you can. A power nap or even just closing your eyes for a few minutes can make a world of difference. Then, if possible, block off a couple of days of no-obligations at the end of the period to focus on regaining your normal sleep and rest rhythms.

Minimize daytime stress

Addressing daytime stress before your head hits the pillow will help with sleep quality. As you know, fellow night-time ruminators, stress can quickly grow from a young sapling to a giant forest. Taking time to wind down before bed, whether it's by talking to your partner or a friend, listening to a meditation, reading a chapter from a (non-stressful) book, or journaling, helps prevent your mind from racing like the Kentucky Derby when you should be resting.

Fueling your body

Jean Anthelme Brillat-Savarin, a French lawyer and politician, said in 1826: *"Tell me what you eat, and I will tell you what you are."*

If you're constantly reaching for greasy fast food with a 64-ounce margarita, your body and energy will feel greasy and drunk. On the other hand, fueling your body with whole, nutrient-dense foods will keep your mind sharp and help you maintain a natural sense of balance throughout your day. You don't need energy drinks and spiked-with-caffeine lemonades if your meals and snacks consist of natural energy-givers like salmon, dark chocolate, green tea, and oats, which can even help reduce anxiety and support overall brain health.

Snacking

Snacking isn't a bad habit on its own—it's *what* you're snacking on that can make or break your energy and your overall health.

My top tip for snacking for balance is this: Stop buying snacks that don't serve you. If unhealthy snacks aren't available, you simply won't eat them. I'm not saying that you can't or shouldn't treat yourself. It's important to indulge occasionally, I mean, I love a rich, delectable brownie like the next person, but keeping your environment stocked with nutritious snacks will make healthier choices the default. Keep healthy snacks like nuts, fruits, and veggies around the office or at home, and you'll naturally reach for better options.

For a full list of foods that increase and decrease energy:

Healthy food habit formation

As I mentioned in the Habits chapter, the best way to remove a habit is to replace it with a different one. As you think about your eating habits, *what is one food that you will replace with a balance-inducing alternative and what will that alternative be?*

Pro Tip: Don't grocery shop on an empty stomach. You'll end up grabbing convenience foods that are more about instant gratification than nourishment. Plan ahead and shop on a full stomach, making it easier to buy what you need, not just what looks good at the moment.

Hydration

Dehydration can make you feel unnecessarily frazzled and sluggish.[33] If you're thirsty, you're already dehydrated. And if your urine is dark, that's another sign you're not drinking enough water.[34] Aim for ½ to 1 ounce of water for every pound you weigh, adjusting for weather and activity level. For example, if you weigh

150 pounds, shoot for 75-150 ounces of water a day. Hate water? Infuse it with cucumber, lemon, or oranges.

Best and worst drinks for balance

The best are:

- Water
- Fruit-infused water
- Coconut water
- Herbal tea

The worst are:

- Coffee (excessive): Too much can cause dehydration, anxiety, and jittery energy.
- Sugary energy drinks: Can you say, sugar crash?
- Alcohol: While appearing to relax you, can disrupt your sleep. In excess, it can lead to addiction, impaired thinking, and embarrassing office stories you don't want to be told about you.

Here are some tips that have worked for myself and my clients to help you drink more water:

- Carry a water bottle and fill it throughout the day.
- Keep a dedicated glass or bottle of water at your desk.
- Keep a full glass or bottle of water next to your bed.
- Switch one can of soda or one cup of coffee for a glass of water or herbal tea.
- Drink small amounts of water often.
- Infuse your water with fruit to make it more exciting.
- If your bottle has a straw lid or pop mouth, keep the straw up and the mouth open. This will limit the number of barriers between you and the water.

Move to thrive

Exercise

I feel lucky that I've always loved moving my body. Whether training for a triathlon or hiking a trail, I thrive on physical challenges. But let's be real—life gets busy, especially with four kids and work demands, even for someone who loves to get her sweat on. And if exercise isn't already your thing, fitting it into a packed schedule can feel impossible. **Everyone knows exercise is good for preventing chronic health conditions. But did you know that it's also a powerful stress reliever?** Exercise reduces stress hormones like cortisol and increases endorphins[35]—the "feel-good" chemicals that boost your mood and help you feel calm.

Plus, regular movement will improve your sleep, creativity, and patience, making you sharper, more collaborative, and more focused at work.[36]

You might be thinking you have no time to work out. Your days are already stacked from 5 a.m. to 7 p.m. every day. **Here's the trick: start small and use your calendar to find gaps in your day.** As we discussed in the Habits chapter, building a new habit is easier when it's bite-sized. You don't need an intense workout every day; you just need to keep moving.

Here are simple ways to fit movement into your day:

- Walk around the block between Zoom calls.
- Stretch in bed before starting your day.
- Park farther away.
- Take a dance break between meetings.
- Turn smaller active moments into workouts (like extending a short walk to pick up the kids or lunges while doing laundry).
- Do a "no-shortcut" workout. For example, find a favorite loop you can hike or run, and put in your calendar, such

as "Canyon Loop" Once you're on the loop, it'll be harder, mentally, to turn around early.

- Join a class. Even better, sign up for a class that has a financial consequence if you cancel or don't show up.

Recovery rules

Recovery is just as important as movement. It allows your body to repair and come back stronger.

Active recovery. There is a concept in the endurance training world called "active recovery." The idea is that after strenuous exercise (unless you're injured) you shouldn't stay sedentary while your body recovers; instead, you should move in a low-key, gentle way. This allows for the muscles to move while also letting them recover and grow stronger.

When I was training for triathlons, I had built-in recovery days. Six days a week were planned training days filled with running, biking, and swimming. One day each week was dedicated to recovery. But instead of using that day to binge-watch *Schitt's Creek*, my coaches told me to go for a walk or do yoga.

Fueling your mind and spirit

Mindfulness

Mindfulness can come across as a little "woo-woo," but all it means is being fully present where you are. The goal of mindfulness is to focus on what's in your immediate surroundings and ignore or avoid distractions. It could be as simple as closing your eyes and thinking about every body part from your toes to your eyebrows, stepping outside and noticing the weather, or listening to all the sounds around you while waiting in line for your morning coffee (or at home waiting for your coffee to brew, looking out the window).

One of the simplest ways to practice mindfulness and reduce stress is with deep breathing. Taking even 60 seconds to focus on your breath can lower your heart rate, release tension, and create a mental reset. Mindful breaks, where you intentionally step away from your screen or workspace to center yourself can provide a powerful reset.

Meditation is another technique that can have lasting effects on your mental well-being. You don't need to dedicate hours to this practice—even a 5-10-minute meditation can make a huge difference in how you handle pressure throughout the day. Guided meditation apps make it easy to do.

Pro Tip: Check with your HR department and people wellness team to see what resources your company provides to support stress management.

Building emotional resilience

When you're burned out and "done," emotions tend to run high. You may find yourself snapping at a waiter who drops your drink, or crying when you notice your dog's collar is broken and you just can't handle another thing going wrong.

Burnout is classic for causing unnecessary, emotionally charged arguments and angst. Learning tools for emotional resilience will help you feel steady even when life gets tough and you're faced with bigger problems than that a restaurant only serves Diet Pepsi and not Diet Coke (I see you soda loyalists).

Identify your triggers. We all have different reactions to situations and stimuli. To begin building resilience, the first step is to recognize what yours are. Perhaps you grew up with parents who weren't there for you when they said they'd be and you often waited outside of school feeling lonely, which led to you now, as an adult, having a sensitivity for people being late. I'm not trying to get all therapist-y on you, but there are real triggers for each of us.

Journaling can help you manage emotions.[37] When you write down your thoughts, it helps you process them, gain clarity, and release tension without drama-dumping or feeling like you're barraging your loved ones with your emotional thought streams. As with most habits, just a few minutes a day can help you clear your mind.

A good talk with a trusted colleague or mentor is another great strategy for balancing your emotions. They can offer guidance, or just listen. Refer to the Communication chapter for healthy ways to begin this conversation.

Other coping mechanisms could include:

- Practicing gratitude for how a situation could be worse.
- Reminding yourself the situation you're in is likely temporary and will pass.

What happens in your body during overwhelm

As we discussed in the Burnout chapter when in a stressful situation or in chronic stress, the body instinctively reacts to keep you safe. Whether under a real-life threat or just the feeling of threat, the body uses all the energy it needs to prepare to fight-flight-or-freeze (aka, freak-out mode and nervous system dysregulation). It's a lot of work–your heart rate increases, breathing quickens, muscles tighten, the release of adrenaline and cortisol, and your blood pressure rises.

In this physiological state of fight-flight-or-freeze, the brain can't function properly because your body's resources are going to your essential organs, focusing on your immediate survival, and not your brain for thoughtful decision-making.[38] It's extra challenging, or even almost impossible, to make thoughtful decisions while in that state.

Remember in the Burnout chapter where I reflected on a situation when I had to fire someone for the first time and it went horribly wrong because of my distressed emotional response? Thankfully, I learned from this experience, and the next time I needed to fire someone (never an easy task but unfortunately comes with the job of running people departments), I prepared myself ahead of time with bullet points and practiced beforehand. Even when my body felt like it was under attack while I said the difficult words I had to say, it didn't influence the conversation; I kept my mind calm and steady. I had come prepared. We can't prevent the body from going into a stress response, but we can prepare for and navigate through it, especially when we know it's coming.

How to regain balance in an overwhelming moment

The first thing to do if your body is in fight-flight-or-freeze, is to ask yourself, *can I survive this? Is it temporary?* The answer is almost always *Yes.* It may suck, but it won't last forever and it won't destroy you.

Then, **use a quick self-care method.** Shift your state with simple actions like repeating to yourself that you're safe while massaging your temples, practicing the box breathing technique described earlier (breathe in for a count of four, hold for four, exhale for four, hold for four), or stepping outside for some fresh air. Do 10 jumping jacks or just close your eyes for two minutes and count your breath.

Here is an additional resource to help you get calm in two minutes or less:

Share big feelings. Big feelings need an outlet. Talking to someone you trust can help release stress. This isn't about venting for sympathy; it's about releasing pressure. Think of your emotions like a balloon. The more you hold in, the more that balloon fills up. Sharing your thoughts and feelings releases some of that pressure, bringing you back to a more manageable state.

Write it down. Dump all your thoughts on a piece of paper or in a private note on your phone—no filters and no judgment. The goal is to clear your mind and create space for new perspectives. Journalling isn't about fixing things in the moment but about freeing yourself from the mental clutter. When you see your thoughts on paper, they lose their hold, and you can process them. Afterward, you might even find that some of those worries weren't as real as they felt in the heat of the moment. When you give your thoughts acknowledgement and space to exist, you can more easily lay them to rest when you close the app or journal.

Acknowledge the negative. Don't chase "happiness." Aiming for 100% happiness isn't realistic. Negative thoughts and feelings are a part of life, and trying to avoid or suppress them never helps, it only makes them louder. The thoughts will come back, bigger and angrier. Thoughts are like children—ignore them, and they'll keep tugging at you until you listen. Once acknowledged and heard, they'll dissipate and move on. And, also like children, thoughts don't need to be correct, they just want to be acknowledged.

Physical movement release. Sometimes, mellow strategies aren't enough to release pent-up stress. That's where physical release comes in. When stress builds up in your body, moving can help shake it out. Whether you go for a run to burn off extra energy, punch a heavy bag, aggressively throw your body around to a Rage Against the Machine song, or simply scream in a private space, it aids in releasing the tension.

When I'm having big feelings, one of my favorite things to do is dance. I blast music (sorry, not sorry, neighbors) and dance my heart out. I don't think about whether the dancing is good or bad, I just move.

If you're pressed for time and need some instant relief, here are a few quick resets:

1. Put your hands on your heart. Close your eyes. And just breathe.
2. Open your hand, palm up, and use the index finger on your other hand to make gentle circles in your palm. Feels good, doesn't it?
3. Bumblebee breathing. This technique quickly calms the nervous system by making a mini sensory deprivation chamber. You do this by placing your finger pads lightly on your head, with the tips of your thumbs pressing into the cartilage of your ear canals, reducing your ability to hear. Then close your eyes and inhale slowly and deeply through your nose and exhale through your nose while making a long, soft humming sound. You will feel the vibrations in your face and throat. Repeat this as often as you can within the time you have. I recommend doing this at least three times in a row and it takes less than a minute to do.

If you're going through an extra-stressful time, like moving into a new home, starting a new job, having a baby, or experiencing a loss, keep in mind that your mental and emotional health needs extra TLC and self-care. And you don't need to have an extraordinarily stressful experience to know that you need a little extra TLC. It may be that you need to activate a company reorganization, hire a new leader for your team, or make a quarterly board presentation. These can all be stressful situations that aren't a part of the daily routine and may require that you give yourself a little extra nurturing. When I trained for triathlons, I had to eat more than usual and go to bed earlier to allow for additional rest and recovery so I could show up well for the next training session.

Setting emotional boundaries

When you're overwhelmed, take a breath and reset before jumping back into the situation that upset you. It's totally appropriate to tell your colleagues that you need a moment to breathe or think. That can look like going outside for some fresh air, taking a walk, or sitting quietly to meditate for two minutes. These micro-moments of pause are self-care. This is how you take care of your needs and prioritize your well-being. After you re-enter, you'll be more available for all that's needed of you.

For example, if you're feeling extra drained ahead of a team excursion, holiday party, or post-work drinks, it's okay to leave early or cancel if you need to recharge. Don't let guilt dictate your actions—your well-being is more important than showing up out of obligation.

If others are disappointed in you for leaving early or not being there, that's their emotion to manage, not yours. All you can do is be as honest, open, and communicative as possible. Sometimes this isn't feasible but more often than not, this won't get you fired or passed up for a promotion by missing one event or leaving one dinner early, especially if these events occur frequently.

Setting emotional boundaries can feel incredibly uncomfortable, but the majority of the time, the short-term discomfort is worth the long-term gain of avoiding burnout. I've had to set these kinds of boundaries many times. There was a recent moment when I was supposed to meet with a colleague for a coffee chat, but I canceled because I knew I wouldn't be fully engaged. I was working on a big presentation and feeling the time pressure of it coming up soon. I told her I wanted to be fully present in our time together but was feeling stressed with the looming presentation. I asked if we could push our coffee date until after that week. She totally understood.

Another time, a teammate called me during a particularly tough day to discuss a project that wasn't going well. I let him know that I was having a challenging day and that I had only a few minutes to connect. I offered to listen for a few minutes now or a longer time later. He said he just needed to vent, I held space to listen and then ended the conversation when my time was up. This kind of boundary doesn't make you less supportive—it makes you more intentional with your energy.

Setting emotional boundaries isn't just about saying "no"; it's about protecting your energy so you can show up fully when it matters most.

Even when someone at work is in crisis, it's still on you to hold your boundaries. You can be kind, but you can't be expected to be everyone's emotional support system at all times. You are responsible for taking care of yourself first, because only then can you show up effectively for everyone else. You are the most important person to take care of, and without those boundaries, you'll be stretched too thin to perform at your best.

Infuse joy

Everyone wants balance so they can enjoy life more. Often you'll hear from those at the end of life, saying they wished they'd enjoyed the journey more and not stressed out as much.[39]

Joy defeats burnout. Not just by reducing stress and overwhelm but by proactively finding, creating, and engaging in moments that bring happiness, laughter, love, and smiles. Like listening to a favorite song. Creating friendships at work. After-work salsa dancing classes. Hiking, camping, golfing, fishing, or other nature activities.

Make sure you have a joyful activity, whether solo or with others scheduled regularly, (weekly or at least once a month) in your calendar to look forward to.

Disconnecting to recharge

In today's always-connected work culture, unplugging, while seemingly impossible, is one of the best ways to maintain your well-being. Setting boundaries with technology allows your brain and body to rest and recharge.

One way to do this is by establishing "no-message zones" or "no-message times." Like putting your phone on "Do Not Disturb" after a certain hour or creating tech-free areas in your home where work can't intrude.

Schedule regular vacations or even mini-breaks throughout the year (without bringing your laptop!) Research shows that time away from work leads to higher productivity, increased creativity, and overall better mental health.[40] Think of a time when you unplugged from work. You set your out-of-office calendar hold, updated and scheduled your vacation responder auto-reply (I love adding a little pizzazz to my OOO message, like "on vacation getting sunburned, I'll reply as soon as I'm done applying aloe when I get back"), closed your computer, and didn't open it again until you were back in work mode. It can take a few days to get into vacation mode, and a few days to get fully back into work mode (I know it's tough with the backlog of emails and messages to wade through). But remember how refreshing it felt to approach your work with fresh eyes, and how grateful you were for the time off?

If you're feeling burnt out right now, there's a high probability you need a break. This is your invitation to schedule your next vacation (however long you can swing it). Get it on the calendar ASAP so you have something to look forward to. If a long vacation isn't in the cards quite yet, even just taking one day off can be helpful for a quick mental health break. You could drive or train someplace close and spend the day in different scenery, or have a "staycation" enjoying what your current city has to offer that you haven't yet explored. Many companies now recognize "mental health" days in addition to vacation and sick time off. Remember, you don't need a 10-day cruise to the Caribbean to honor this type of self-care.

Hobbies and passions

Engaging in hobbies outside of work isn't just a "nice-to-have"—it's mandatory for maintaining a balanced life. Whether it's painting, gardening, or playing in a local sports team, you're giving your mind a break from work-related stress.

Creative hobbies can redirect your stressed-out thoughts. It's hard to feel stressed when you're coloring a mandala of a puppy. I've never met a well-balanced executive who didn't have a pleasurable activity outside of work, whether it was golf, surfing, cooking, puzzles, volunteering, or knitting. Inspiration from these activities can also make you better at your work. I've been inspired countless times by the books I read or the artistic endeavors I enjoy.

What's great about hobbies is that there is no motive other than pure enjoyment. The goal isn't to get better but to simply do something that brings you joy. And you don't have to spend hours and hours doing it; sometimes 15 minutes does the trick.

If you're having trouble making your hobby a priority, try joining a group of fellow hobbyists. In addition to being around people with similar interests, you can build accountability partnerships with them, make new friends, and check in on how you are all coming along with your pursuits.

Practical self-care routines

Most of my clients, and almost every burned-out professional I speak with, tend to miss multiple—or all—of what I call the "Brilliant Basics" of self-care. Burnout is rarely caused by just one thing, and it's rarely *just* about work. It's influenced by a combination of lifestyle choices, both in and outside the workplace. By ensuring your basic self-care needs are met, you significantly reduce the chances of burning out.

These basics aren't groundbreaking, but they are profound in their simplicity. They're so basic, in fact, that they're often overlooked, and they are the first to be let go when new tasks and priorities show up. And that's what makes them challenging to stick to. Simple doesn't mean easy. It takes intention and effort to add self-care into your daily routine and sustain it.

The "Brilliant Basics" cover how we treat our minds and bodies, and you can remember them through the acronym CHEER:

C - Connection

Connecting to the parts of yourself that go beyond your work roles and responsibilities. Connect with friends, nature, or your spirituality—anything that makes you feel part of something bigger than yourself.

H - Hydration

Your body can go weeks without food but only a few days without water.[41] Don't let something as simple as drinking water be the reason you're running on fumes.

E - Eating to Nourish

Nourish your body with food that fuels it (see the above section on fueling your body for ideas). Don't allow yourself to make a habit of working through lunch or grazing on unhealthy vending machine snacks all day because you're too focused.

E - Exercise

We are not built to sit for hours on end. Whether it's a morning workout or a quick walk at lunch, movement will lead to more balance.

R - Rest

Rest is twofold: it includes both sleep and intentional moments of downtime during the day. Consistent, quality sleep is crucial, but you also need those mini breaks—whether it's stepping outside for fresh air, or just pausing for a brain break. Yes, I sound like a broken record about this, but there's a reason for it, and there's a reason labor laws mandate breaks—it's because our bodies and minds need them to function at their best.

Morning rituals for success

What you do in the morning sets the tone for the entire day. Whether it's a routine you do right after you wake up or what you do when you get to your desk, these rituals can prime you for success.

Here are some ideas:

- **Check-In:** Before you get out of bed (or at least before starting the tasks of your day), pause for a moment, take a deep breath, and ask, *"How am I doing right now? What's my weather report?"*

  - **Notice your:**

    - **Emotions** - *How's my heart feeling? What is my predominant emotion?* Notice your emotional state heading into the day without any judgment or need to change it.

    - **Body** - *What's going on in my body?* Do a scan. Is there any discomfort or tension? *What are the sensations?* Again, just notice and acknowledge without a solution at this point. Approach yourself with compassion and curiosity.

- **Mind** - *What's the current state of my mind? Are my thoughts clear or hazy? Rushing ahead to the future or in the moment?* Acknowledge, without judgment, what's going on in your mind.

- **Figure out what you need today to take care of your whole self.** *Which of the "Brilliant Basics" do I need to focus on today that will support my current state and help me thrive? Connection? Movement? Rest?*

- **Set your intention for the day.** Take a moment to think about how you want to set yourself up for success today. *What mindset and energy do I want to anchor for the day ahead?* Write your intention on a Post-it or put it into your calendar to remind you during the day. (**Pro tip:** Set up an alarm notification on your phone or computer with your intention as a reminder during the day to reset yourself. It's especially helpful on extra stressful days when you forget your intention.)

Example intentions:

"I keep an open mind and curious mindset."
"I breathe before making decisions."
"I think about the long and short-term impact of my choices."

- **Meditation or mindfulness**: Start your day with a few minutes of quiet to center yourself. You can use an app for guided meditation, or simply set a timer and sit in silence.
- **Journaling**: Before getting into your day, allow yourself to release all thoughts that are weighing on your mind.
- **Stretching**: Gently wake up your body with some stretches. Feel how good it is to expand and contract, and maybe even give yourself a strong and deep squeeze at the end.

- **Mindful breakfast**: Eat a nutritious breakfast without distractions. Take your time, notice how you chew your food, and sip your coffee or tea. Enjoy the moment and anchor yourself for the day ahead.
- **Natural sunlight:** If you can, expose yourself to natural sunlight first thing in the morning. This helps activate brain chemicals that promote wakefulness and set your body's internal clock.

Midday reset strategies

I don't know about you, but after hours of chugging along, I get pretty fatigued. Around midday, I start looking for comfy napping spots or crave something sweet in an effort to keep me going. Instead of resorting to the closest candy bar, here are some more productive ways to reset and recharge:

- **Move your body:** Take a walk, whether around the building, going up and down some stairs, or outside. If you're able, do some push-ups or jumping jacks to get the blood flowing.
- **Go outside:** Getting away from your desk and breathing some fresh air works wonders as a little recharge. Just thinking about feeling fresh air in my lungs and on my skin is energizing.
- **Breathing exercises**: Practice box breathing (described above) or other deep breathing methods, like the 4,7,8 technique– inhale for four seconds, hold for seven, and exhale for eight seconds.
- **Quiet moments**: Take just a few minutes away from screens and other intrusive noises and attention grabbers, and just be.
- **Hydrate with intention**: Step away from your desk and refill your water bottle or get some herbal tea. This intentional moment is perfect for giving your brain a much-needed pause.

- **Send a note to a friend or family member**: Take a moment to think of someone you care about or appreciate and send them a quick text or voice note just to let them know you're thinking of them. Not only have you added a little delight to their day, but if you get a thoughtful note back, then you get a double win of good feelings.

Evening wind-down practices

How we end our days are just as impactful as how we start them. Create an evening routine to help you decompress, close the day, and prepare for a restful and restorative sleep. I've tried lots of different rituals over the years, and just like everything else, my evening routine evolves as I do.

My current wind-down routine includes finishing dinner three hours before bedtime, prepping the kids' snacks, lunches, and morning vitamins, drinking herbal tea, skin and oral care while listening to an audiobook, journalling, some gentle stretching, and raising my legs against a wall for ten minutes (which I've read helps lessen anxiety, increase circulation and gets your body ready for snoozing[42]) before getting into bed. Other rituals that could be a part of your evening wind-down are: debriefing the day with your partner or friend, reading a book, doing a crossword, gratitude journaling, and taking a warm bath or shower.

Just like everything else, try different rituals and see what supports you best.

Overcoming common self-care obstacles

Time constraints

One of the most common reasons someone neglects themselves I hear is, "I don't have time for self-care." But as we have already proven throughout this chapter, you don't need a huge block of time to take care of yourself. Focus on quality over quantity. A few intentional minutes of focus on you and your care will have lasting effects when done consistently. Find the micro-moments in your day—like your commute, lunch break, or the minutes you have between meetings—and use them for self-care. It's not about adding another to-do; it's about finding and capitalizing on the small moments you already have in your existing schedule to intentionally recharge.

Just like in the Efficiency chapter when we talked about clarity around priorities informing what gets your time and attention, we use this same strategy with self-care. With authentic and sustainable self-care in mind, you can more easily make decisions that support quality and systemic self-care. This might look like declining lunch with a colleague so that you can read a book or go for a walk in silence, or saying no to an after-work event because you want to watch an episode of your favorite show while wearing a face mask and wake up early the next morning to do a sunrise yoga class. It could even be as simple as choosing to step away from your desk for 10 minutes to take a walk instead of powering through reviewing the remaining stack of resumes. **It's not always about time management; it's about priority management**. Self-care deserves a place on your priority list.

Guilt

If we haven't debunked this already, this should convince you that taking time for self-care is indulgent or selfish, nor is it a luxury—it's a necessity. If you want to show up as your best at work, at home, and everywhere else, the best way to do that is to make sure that you take care of your mind, body, and spirit. Prioritizing your well-being is an investment in your long-term success.

If you don't take care of yourself, how can you expect to show up the best way you can for the people who need you most? If you don't do it for you, do it for the people watching you. If you have children, you are role-modeling what a healthy relationship with the self looks like. How you take care of yourself is creating the model for how your children will take care of themselves as they grow older. If you want your children to become adults who prioritize their well-being, then you have to show them how by doing it yourself.

Staying consistent

Now that you know why self-care is important and how to build it into your days, the last piece of the self-care puzzle is being consistent. We talked about the importance of consistency in the habits chapter, so I won't bore you by reiterating it all. But what I will say is that for self-care to become a habit and have a lasting influence on your balance and well-being, just like any other habit, you have to be consistent with it. It's easy to start strong and then let your practice slip when life gets hectic. Here's how you can stay on track:

- **Set reminders**: Use your phone or calendar to schedule self-care breaks and alerts throughout the day.
- **Track your progress**: Whether it's keeping a journal or using an app, track your self-care habits to help you stay accountable and recognize what's working.
- **Adjust as needed**: Your self-care routines and practices aren't set in stone. As life and work demands change, so should your approach to self-care. Be flexible and make adjustments to ensure your self-care evolves with you.

Flexibility in self-care

Life will always try to thwart the time you have for yourself. There are always choices to make with how you spend your time.

When plans go awry, like one of your kids is up sick all night, or your flow gets derailed by an unexpected call from your boss in the middle of a deep strategy thinking session, or chaos strikes like when my dishwasher spontaneously combusted and flooded our kitchen and living room, resulting in months of disruption with demolition, research, and installation of flooring, your self-care will—and can—need to be flexible.

For example, maybe you always go for a run after dinner, but this morning, your car broke down and you had to power walk two miles to get to the mechanic. You could adjust your evening routine to be more low-key, maybe you do some yoga or go for a walk instead of a run. Or maybe it was an emotionally stressful day and you invite a friend over to catch up over a beer and pizza delivery instead of cooking the new recipe you had planned. **There are ways to nurture yourself, even in the hardest of moments. You can shift your self-care to match the circumstances and type of energy you need.**

Self-care wrap-up

Regular self-care is a way to add energy back into your reserves so you can maintain homeostasis more often. When you practice self-care your reserves won't be as depleted when you come out of stressful situations because you've been regularly refueling and being kind to yourself.

You'll also be able to more easily *respond* thoughtfully rather than react impulsively, and take care of issues when they're small, before they grow.

Consistent and sustainable self-care ensures you are cared for and won't get overly depleted. You'll be able to let go of resenting that no one else is making you a priority. You can take care of your basic human needs, and from a place of fulfillment and calm (through movement, nutrition, hydration, rest, recovery, and emotional well-being practices), you'll notice a stronger, calmer, more resilient you.

✓ **Self-care isn't a one-time event.** It's a lifelong practice.

✓ **You don't need to spend lots of time or money to reap the benefits of self-care.** It's about taking care of your basic needs to fulfill your mind, body, and spirit.

✓ **Adjust your self-care routines based on the flow of your day.** Just don't make it a practice to skip what's essential.

✓ **If all else fails in a day, revert to the brilliant basics of self-care.** CHEER (Connection, Hydration, Exercise, Eating, and Rest).

✓ **Modeling self-care will help all those around you.** Which will also improve your balance.

You have everything needed to activate sustainable and systemic self-care into your days, and are ready to put out the flames of burnout once and for all.

Now we'll close up with a brief conclusion and set you on your way.

Conclusion

Here we are, wrapping up our time together!

We've covered a lot of ground. My goal for you is not to be overwhelmed by all the tools and tips. You can **start small** with the first area that speaks to you, and tackle one concept at a time.

As you've been reading, the path to a more balanced life is guided by being efficient with your time and energy, creating small healthy habits, communicating effectively, harnessing your community, and taking care of yourself. It's as simple (and sometimes as difficult) as that.

Give yourself permission to be a work in progress. No one is perfect. I'm not perfect, and I have no desire to strive for perfection. Perfection is fleeting, unsustainable, and unrealistic. But progress! Progress is different. Anyone can achieve progress. Anyone can get an A+ on progress. And as high-performers, you and I love getting A+s.

As we mentioned at the beginning of the book, **balance does *not* mean that all areas of your life will suddenly be equal.** Look at your life like a pie. Balance is ensuring all the slices—no matter how big each one is on a day-to-day basis—of your life fit. Some pieces will be bigger and others will be smaller, based on what's happening at any given moment. But the pie should *always* include *the nurturing of you*. That is not negotiable.

One day a research project, operations crisis, or employee reviews might need the majority of your attention. On a different day, a loved one might need more of your attention than usual. Sometimes, urgent demands all hit at once, and to retain balance you'll lean on your daily self-care rituals (Remember to CHEER! See Self-Care chapter).

Balance is a state of being, where work stress no longer regularly disrupts your personal time, mood, social life, relationships, or health, which all suffer when you're in chronic stress. Your stressed self is never going to be your best self.[43]

It takes courage to make a change and move out of your comfort zone, especially if your comfort zone is ironically a stress-out one.

Change can feel uncomfortable because it's new. Courage is needed to change. If it was easy, you'd be doing it already. But you do have all the courage you need to make the transformation you seek.

Bonus: Doing this courageous work will set the stage for others to do the same. Your colleagues will feel inspired and allowed to do the same, leading to a much healthier team and company. Fostering balance within yourself is not selfish, it is a giving act for others as well.

Becoming a "yogi master" of balance

Achieving balance doesn't mean that everything in life will be steady and still. There will always be movement, surprises, chaos, changes, issues, and stress around you, both positive and negative.

Creating balance is about having all the muscles you need to remain calm and steady while all the moving takes place. Balancing is an active act. Take yoga for example. In yoga, you may appear still while holding a pose, but in actuality so much

168 | Burnout to Balance

is moving and you are never stagnant. While holding a pose, even one where you look completely still and balanced, your body is actively flexing and releasing tiny and large muscles to keep you in the pose. It's actively working to balance, never not moving, never stagnant.

When you practice the concepts in this book, you will work the muscles and coordination needed to hold a metaphorical headstand like a yogi master. And when life goes into a whirl, and stress presents itself, as it does every day, you'll have the confidence to rely on those muscles to keep you stable. This confidence will create emotional and physiological steadiness and calm.

And if you need some extra support to get a jump start on balance and moving forward with the changes you want to make, whether for yourself or to help prevent burnout across the whole organization, Be Courageous and I are here to help.

I'm rooting for you. You're welcome to email me at balance@ bcrgs.com, direct message, or connect with me on LinkedIn at https://www.linkedin.com/in/jennahermans.

As the closing credits roll, here's a quick high-level reminder of what you learned.

Recap of *Burnout to Balance* strategies

1. Efficiency

√ Having systems for task management can transform a chaotic schedule into a manageable one, allowing for better prioritization, reduced stress, and higher productivity.

√ Utilize your calendar to help manage both professional and personal responsibilities. If it isn't in the calendar, it doesn't exist.

✓ Continuously seek ways to improve your workflow and create a streamlined approach to help prevent burnout and make it easier to be present and engaged both at work and home.

✓ Recognize and respect your natural energy cycles, take regular breaks, and set boundaries to sustain high performance.

2. Habits

✓ Motivation is unreliable due to its natural fluctuations. Build habits to ensure consistency and progress even on low-energy days.

✓ Create micro-habits that are easy to accomplish, which help establish a foundation for sustainable routines. Small, consistent actions lead to significant, long-term results.

✓ Use triggers and rituals to support habit formation by priming your mind and environment. This makes habits easier to initiate and maintain, reinforcing consistency over time.

✓ Share your goals with others and plan for potential setbacks to maintain commitment. Recognizing and addressing resistance prevents slips from turning into long-term slides.

3. Communication

✓ Be clear and intentional to reduce misunderstandings, foster efficiency, and maintain balance. This helps prevent the frustration of repeated explanations and misunderstandings that can contribute to burnout.

✓ Be proactive when asking for support to avoid last-minute stress and ensure smoother collaboration and task execution.

✓ Assertive communication is the best approach to foster clear, respectful communication. It encourages setting boundaries, making requests, and delegating tasks in a way that maintains mutual respect and collaboration.

✓ Engage in active listening and simplify messages to minimize information overload, enhance understanding, and prevent stress caused by miscommunication and decision fatigue.

4. Community

✓ Build strong, supportive relationships; a trusted work community helps lighten emotional loads, provides assistance during high-pressure times, and fosters resilience.

✓ Connect with colleagues for advice, collaboration, or just to vent to reduce stress. Knowing someone has your back can make overwhelming tasks feel more manageable and prevent work stress from seeping into personal life.

✓ Assess and nurture relationships that contribute positively to your well-being. This may involve creating distance from those who drain your energy and investing time with those who uplift and support you.

✓ A well-rounded community, including mentors, peers, and personal support networks, helps buffer against burnout and contributes to overall balance. Share parts of your life, participate in team-building, and even seek external help like therapy to strengthen resilience and improve mental health.

5. Self-Care

✓ Self-care is necessary for showing up as your best self at work and in life, to prevent burnout and sustain energy for long-term well-being.

✓ Effective, sustainable, and systemic self-care involves integrating small, manageable habits into daily routines rather than expensive, occasional indulgences, ensuring long-lasting balance and rejuvenation.

✓ Regular self-care enhances mental clarity and efficiency, debunking the myth that it is unproductive. A well-rested, balanced person is more effective and produces higher-quality work in less time.

✓ Self-care routines need to be adaptable to life's disruptions. Be proactive and consistent, yet flexible, to maintain well-being even during challenging or unexpected circumstances.

YOUR PATH TO BALANCE

- Write down the key concepts that resonated with you. Revisit this list periodically to keep it fresh in your mind.
- Write down one small thing you want to activate now.
- Write down what you need to be able to activate that small thing.
- How will you own your balance, right now, and into the future?
- Download the free *Burnout to Balance Action Plan* here:

Acknowledgements

I first want to acknowledge (not in a "thank-you" way, but in a "we need to change this" way) our society's current work culture, which celebrates hyper-productivity and over-extension. It's currently seen as a badge of honor to say, *"I barely sleep because I'm working so hard."* This is an unsustainable and harmful way of life. *Working hard* is admirable; *self-sacrifice* should not be revered.

This book was inspired by the numerous requests by many readers who asked for a business version of *Chaos to Calm* because parenting and working are two roles that bring the most stress in our adult life journeys.

To everyone who requested this book, thank you for trusting me and my approach to live a more balanced, calm, and intentional life.

To my husband, Kyle, to whom this book is dedicated, I couldn't ask for a more amazing life partner. I am endlessly grateful for your support of this book and every other project and venture I take on. You bring balance to my world.

To Shannon, I wouldn't have been able to make this book if not for you. Your partnership was invaluable, from project management and editing to thought partnership and keeping me on track, and so much more.

To my colleagues, clients, and friends, I don't take for granted your openness, insights, and sharing of your stories, hardships, and challenges, both in and out of the workplace. Your contributions gave life to this book.

To my past employers and employees, I'm grateful for all of the learning I experienced and earned from working with you. The lessons were invaluable and created the foundation of the leader, coach, and professional I am today and the perspectives I bring to my life, both professionally and personally.

Readers, I'd love to hear from you. Please reach out to me via LinkedIn or email:

LinkedIn: https://www.linkedin.com/in/jennahermans
Email: balance@bcrgs.com

Other books by Jenna Hermans:

Chaos to Calm: Five Ways Busy Parents Can Break Free From Overwhelm, available everywhere.

References

1   World Health Organization. (2019). Burn-out an "occupational phenomenon": International Classification of Diseases. Retrieved from WHO Website.

2   Deloitte. (2018). Workplace burnout survey. Retrieved from Deloitte Insights.

3   American Psychological Association. (2020). "Stress in America 2020: A National Mental Health Crisis."

4   Arnsten, A. F. T. (2009). "Stress signalling pathways that impair prefrontal cortex structure and function." Nature Reviews Neuroscience, 10(6), 410-422. doi:10.1038/nrn2648.

5   Csikszentmihalyi, M., & LeFevre, J. (1989). Optimal experience in work and leisure. Journal of Personality and Social Psychology, 56(5), 815-822.

6   Wahbeh, H., Calabrese, C., Zwickey, C., & Zajdel, B. (2007). Binaural Auditory Beats Affect Vigilance Performance and Mood. Physiology & Behavior, 92(4), 623-627. doi:10.1016/j.physbeh.2007.05.024

7   Mark, G., Gudith, D., & Klocke, U. (2008). The cost of interrupted work: More speed and stress. Proceedings of the SIGCHI Conference on Human Factors in Computing Systems, 107–110. https://doi.org/10.1145/1357054.1357072

8   Evaluating the Connection between Thermal Comfort and Productivity in Buildings: A Systematic Literature Review by Ana Maria Bueno,Antonio Augusto de Paula Xavier, and Evandro Eduardo Broday

9   Browning, M. H. E. M., & Lee, K. (2019). The impact of nature on employee mental health and well-being: A systematic review of the evidence. Environmental Research, 176, 108632.

10   Series: Elements in Applied Evolutionary Science, Publisher: Cambridge University Press, Print publication: 18 May 2023

11   Ulrich, R. S. (1984). View through a window may influence recovery from surgery. Science, 224(4647), 420-421. doi:10.1126/science.6143402

12   Walker, M. P. (2017). Why We Sleep: Unlocking the Power of Sleep and Dreams. Scribner.

13   Baglioni, C., Battagliese, G., Feige, B., Spiegelhalder, K., Nissen, C., Voderholzer, U., ... & Riemann, D. (2011). "Insomnia as a predictor of depression: A meta-analytic evaluation of longitudinal epidemiological studies." Sleep Medicine Reviews, 15(4), 231-238.

14   O'Connor, P. J., Herring, M. P., & Carvalho, A. (2010). "Mental health benefits of strength training in adults." American Journal of Lifestyle Medicine, 4(5), 377-396. doi:10.1177/1559827610368771.

15   Puetz, T. W., Flowers, S. S., & O'Connor, P. J. (2008). "A randomized controlled trial of the effects of aerobic exercise on feelings of energy and fatigue in sedentary adults." Psychotherapy and Psychosomatics, 77(3), 167-174.

16   Axelsson, J., Ingre, M., Åkerstedt, T., & Holmback, U. (2005). "Effects of sleep deprivation on circadian rhythms of testosterone and cortisol in healthy men." Journal of Endocrinology, 183(1), 145-154. doi:10.1677/joe.1.06284.

17   "Executive Control of Cognitive Processes in Task Switching" by Joshua S. Rubinstein, David E. Meyer, and Jeffrey E. Evans. This study was published in 2001 in the Journal of Experimental Psychology: Human Perception and Performance.)

18   Baumeister, R. F., & Tierney, J. (2011). Willpower: Rediscovering the Greatest Human Strength.

19   Kim, S., & Wadhwa, M. (2020). Taking a break: How breaks during work and study improve productivity, creativity, and focus. Journal of Behavioral Science, 26(2), 105-112.

20   Rosekind, M. R., Gander, P. H., Miller, D. L., Gregory, K. B., Smith, R. M., Weldon, K. J., Co, E. L., McNally, K. L., & Lebacqz, J. V. (1995). "Napping to protect against the deleterious effects of sleep deprivation." Sleep, 18(7), 581-591.

21   Fogg, B.J. (2019). Tiny Habits: The Small Changes That Change Everything. Houghton Mifflin Harcourt.

22   Christakis, N. A., & Fowler, J. H. (2007). The spread of obesity in a large social network over 32 years. New England Journal of Medicine, 357(4), 370-379. https://doi.org/10.1056/NEJMsa066082

23   The Relationship Between Workplace Stressors and Mortality and Health Costs in the United States, By Joel Goh, Jeffrey, Pfeffer, Stefanos Zenios. Management Science March 13, 2016 Vol. 62, Issue 2, Pages 608-628.

24   Dolan, R. J., & Dayan, P. (2013). Goals and habits in the brain. Neuron, 80(2), 312-325

25   Hiatt, J. M. (2006). ADKAR: A Model for Change in Business, Government, and Our Community. Prosci Research.

26   Mehrabian, A. (1971). Silent Messages. Wadsworth Publishing Company.

27   Baumeister, R. F., & Leary, M. R. (1995). The need to belong: Desire for interpersonal attachments as a fundamental human motivation. Psychological Bulletin, 117(3), 497-529. doi:10.1037/0033-2909.117.3.497

28   Workplace Insight. (2019). Half of people have quit their job due to poor relationship with their boss Robert Half. (2020). *The 6 Main Causes of Unhappy Staff and Job Dissatisfaction.*

29   American Psychological Association (APA). (2021). The role of workplace support in managing stress and fostering resilience.

30   Centers for Disease Control and Prevention. (2014). Short sleep duration among U.S. adults. Morbidity and Mortality Weekly Report (MMWR), 63(8), 37-41.

31   Chang, A.-M., Aeschbach, D., Duffy, J. F., & Czeisler, C. A. (2015). "Evening use of light-emitting eReaders negatively affects sleep, circadian timing, and next-morning alertness." Proceedings of the National Academy of Sciences, 112(4), 1232-1237. doi:10.1073/pnas.1418490112.

32   Figueiro, M. G., & Rea, M. S. (2010). "Lack of short-wavelength light during the school day delays dim light melatonin onset (DLMO) in middle school students." Neuro Endocrinology Letters, 31(1), 92-96.

33   Ganio, M. S., Armstrong, L. E., Casa, D. J., McDermott, B. P., Lee, E. C., Yamamoto, L. M., ... & Maresh, C. M. (2011). Mild dehydration impairs cognitive performance and mood of men. Physiology & Behavior, 102(3-4), 290-296.

34   Popkin, B. M., D'Anci, K. E., & Rosenberg, I. H. (2010). Water, hydration, and health. Nutrition Reviews, 68(8), 439-458.

35   Weir, K. (2011). The exercise effect. Monitor on Psychology, 42(11), 48–52.39

36   Chang, Y. K., Labban, J. D., Gapin, J. I., & Etnier, J. L. (2012). "The effects of acute exercise on cognitive performance: A meta-analysis." Brain Research, 1453, 87-101. doi:10.1016/j.brainres.2012.02.068.

37   Pennebaker, J. W., & Beall, S. K. (1986). "Confronting a traumatic event: Toward an understanding of inhibition and disease." Journal of Abnormal Psychology, 95(3), 274-281. doi:10.1037/0021-843X.95.3.274.

38   Arnsten, A. F. T. (2009). "Stress signalling pathways that impair prefrontal cortex structure and function." Nature Reviews Neuroscience, 10(6), 410-422. doi:10.1038/nrn2648.

39   Seiter, T. (2023, December 12). How to live: What the dying tell us. Psychology Today. https://www.psychologytoday.com/us/blog/mindful-relationships/202312/how-to-live-what-the-dying-tell-us

40   Fritz, C., & Sonnentag, S. (2006). "Recovery, well-being, and performance-related outcomes: The role of workload and vacation experiences." Journal of Applied Psychology, 91(4), 936-945. doi:10.1037/0021-9010.91.4.936.

41   Moritz, W.J. (1947). "The Influence of Hydration on Human Survival." Archives of Criminology.

42   Caldwell, K., Harrison, M., Adams, M., & Triplett, N. T. (2011). Effect of restorative yoga vs. stretching on anxiety and sleep quality in veterans. Sleep Health, 7(4), 379-388.

43   Geher, G. (2020, December 12). Your stressed self vs. your best self. Psychology Today. https://www.psychologytoday.com/us/blog/darwins-subterranean-world/202012/your-stressed-self-vs-your-best-self

www.ingramcontent.com/pod-product-compliance
Lightning Source LLC
Chambersburg PA
CBHW061756120626
46550CB00005B/2014